S0-AYZ-291

Tara.

TE-TAO CHING

For
Tara — Graduation 1995

— "When the doors of perception are
cleansed, things will appear as
they truly 'are'"
             — williams Blake.

If you know that you know nothing,
every door has light piercing through
the cracks. Go to them.

                    Love always
                    Christa

TE-TAO CHING

LAO-TZU

TRANSLATED FROM THE MA-WANG-TUI TEXTS,
WITH AN INTRODUCTION AND COMMENTARY,
BY ROBERT G. HENRICKS

THE MODERN LIBRARY
NEW YORK

1993 Modern Library Edition

Translation and new text copyright © 1989 by Robert G. Henricks

All rights reserved under International and Pan-American
Copyright Conventions. Published in the United States by
Random House, Inc., New York, and simultaneously in Canada by
Random House of Canada Limited, Toronto.

This work was originally published in hardcover by Ballantine Books,
a division of Random House, Inc., in 1989.

Grateful acknowledgment is made to Macmillan Publishing Company
for permission to quote excerpts from *The Way of Lao Tzu* by
Wing-Tsit Chan. Copyright © 1963 by Macmillan Publishing Company.
Reprinted by permission.

Jacket portrait courtesy of The Bettmann Archive

Printed on recycled, acid-free paper.

Library of Congress Cataloging-in-Publication Data
Lao-tzu.
    [Tao te ching. English]
    Lao-tzu: Te-tao ching: a new translation based on the recently
discovered Ma-wang-tui texts/translated, with an introduction and
commentary, by Robert G. Henricks.
    p.   cm.
Includes bibliographical references.
    ISBN 0-679-60060-4
    I. Henricks, Robert G. 1943   . II. Title.
BL1900.L26E5   1993
299'.51482 dc20   93-15015

Manufactured in the United States of America

2 4 6 8 9 7 5 3 1

For Herrlee Glessner Creel

*Who will undoubtedly disagree with my
interpretation of the* Lao-tzu *but whose
strong support of my work on the Ma-wang-tui
texts has meant a great deal.*

CONTENTS

PREFACE

In the winter of 1976 I read through the Ma-wang-tui texts of *Lao-tzu* with a colleague and two students and immediately, and excitedly, had thoughts of doing a translation. The following year, doctoral dissertation out of the way, I began to study the texts seriously, being initially interested in determining how they differed from later texts of the *Lao-tzu* and why. One project seemed to lead to another, such that over the years I ended up publishing no less than ten articles on the texts, the original thought of doing a translation now far from my mind.

I was delighted, therefore, to receive a phone call from Owen Lock, editor in chief of Del Rey Books (an imprint of Ballantine Books), in November 1986, asking whether I might be interested in translating the Ma-wang-tui texts for popular consumption. Giving the matter some thought, I soon saw that this would give me the opportunity to bring to a completion in some ways the previous work I had done on the texts; at the same time, this makes available for the general readership the latest knowledge we have of this important text in Taoism.

I am indebted to Owen Lock for having the foresight to realize the significance of this project and for his support of and belief in my work. I also owe much to my good friend Richard Gotshalk, who first urged me to look into this text many years ago. Dick and I have had many long talks together over the years about the philosophy of this text, and he carefully read through my first draft translation and introduction and suggested a number of important changes and different ways in which the text might be read. Finally I want to thank my colleague at Dartmouth, Li Hua-yüan Mowry, who kindly, as she has done on many occasions before, went over a number of troubling passages in the text with me, sharing with me her sense of the text from the point of view of a native speaker.

INTRODUCTION

Specialists on Chinese religion and thought find it useful to distinguish, initially at least, between the Taoist religion on the one hand and philosophical Taoism on the other. We agree in dating the formal beginning of the Taoist religion to the establishment of the Celestial Master Sect, c. A.D. 150, by a man named Chang Taoling; philosophical Taoism is best represented for us in the thought of two texts written in early China, one called the *Chuang-tzu*, which preserves the ideas of the philosopher Chuang Chou (fl. 350–320 B.C.), the other an anonymous product known as the *Lao-tzu* (which means "the Old Master" or "Old Philosopher") or the *Tao-te ching (The Book of the Way and Its Power)*. The *Lao-tzu*, like the *Chuang-tzu*, probably represents currents of thought in China around 300 B.C., though by tradition the *Lao-tzu* was written by a contemporary of Confucius named Li Erh, Confucius' dates being 551–479 B.C.[1]

There are many similar ideas in the texts of *Lao-tzu* and *Chuang-tzu*; there are major differences between the two texts as well. For example, a good part of the *Lao-tzu* is addressed to the man who would be king and is concerned with the correct, Taoist way to rule; Chuang-tzu has no interest in social-political matters. Chuang-tzu's message is addressed to the rugged individualist who turns his back on social commitment in his search for the fulfilled life. There are also major differences between the two books in style. The *Chuang-tzu* is composed of thirty-three chapters, each chapter a mixture of philosophic discourse, anecdote, fable, and tale, stories filled with delightful, unforgettable characters.[2] The *Lao-tzu*, by contrast, has a total of eighty-one chapters, each one being more like a poem in form.

I. THE MA-WANG-TUI TEXTS

A number of extraordinary textual discoveries have been made by archaeologists in China in the last twenty years, those discoveries providing the reason, and the materials, for the present translation series. At Yin-ch'üeh-shan in Shantung, for example, portions of a number of early philosophical texts—including the *Kuan-tzu*, the *Yen-tzu ch'un-ch'iu*, and the militarist treatises *Sun Pin ping-fa* and *Sun Wu ping-fa* (i.e., *Sun-tzu's Art of War*)—have been unearthed; while at Shui-hu-ti in Hupeh archaeologists found, among other things, materials relating to a Ch'in (221–207 B.C.) code of law.[3]

Of greatest significance to date, a tremendous discovery was made in the last months of 1973 in south-central China near Changsha (Hunan Province) in the small village of Ma-wang-tui. In Han Tomb No. 3 at Ma-wang-tui, the grave of the son of a man named Li Ts'ang, Li Ts'ang having been marquis of Tai and prime minister of Changsha in early Han dynasty times,* archaeologists discovered a rich cache of funerary goods including a large group of texts. An inventory slip in the tomb informs us that this man was buried on the equivalent in the Western calendar of April 4, 168 B.C., thus providing a *terminus ante quem* for these materials. But more precise dating is possible in some cases based on the style of the calligraphy used and the practice of taboo-name avoidance—the personal name of an emperor in ancient China was not to be used in texts copied during his reign (more on these matters below).

A total of fifty-one items have been identified in the find by Chinese specialists working on the materials; most of these are written on silk, though a few are recorded on slips of bamboo and/or wood. Though most of the materials found are texts, there are maps, charts, and diagrams among the finds as well.† The importance of these materials to our understanding of early Chinese philosophy, history, literature, political thought, scientific thought, etc., was recognized right from the start and can hardly be overestimated.

There are texts on medical theories and practices, texts on Yin and Yang and the Five Elements (or "Phases"—*wu-hsing*), texts on political philosophy, and texts on astronomy and astrology. The medical treatises treat such matters as the conduits of the circulatory system, the fatal signs exhibited by these

---

*The dates of the former Han dynasty were 206 B.C.–A.D. 5.

†One map shows troop deployment in and around Changsha in the early Han. One of the charts illustrates forty-four positions assumed in therapeutic calisthenics *(tao-yin)*, the kinds of exercise that were later to play a prominent role in Taoist longevity techniques.

conduits, remedies and prescriptions for fifty-two diseases *(Wu-shih-erh ping-fang)*, childbirth, methods for nourishing life, and the benefits of grain avoidance in diet. One of the medical treatises may in fact be the long lost *Huang-ti wai-ching (External Classic of the Yellow Emperor)*. The texts on astronomy and astrology are mainly concerned with good and bad omens. One of these plots the orbits of five planets for the years 246–177 B.C.: this is called *Prognostications Related to the Five Planets (Wu-hsing chan)*. Another illustrated scroll called *Prognostications Related to Astronomical and Meteorological Phenomena (T'ien-wen ch'i-hsiang chan)* has twenty-nine vivid drawings of comets. Needless to say, these are extremely important materials for tracing the development of astronomy in early China.

One of the Ma-wang-tui texts contains anecdotal material similar to what we now find in the *Tso-chuan*, recording historical events in the Spring and Autumn (Ch'un-ch'iu) period in China (722–481 B.C.). Also found was an early version of the *Chan-kuo ts'e (Intrigues of the Warring States)*, a version with a total of twenty-seven chapters, sixteen of these not previously seen, all of this providing new information on the history of this important age (c. 480–222 B.C.).

Most of the texts found at Ma-wang-tui are documents of which we had no prior knowledge, though in some cases we knew of the item by name. Most significant in this regard, perhaps, are the texts being identified as the lost *Huang-ti ssu-ching (Four Classics of the Yellow Emperor)*. The *Four Classics of the Yellow Emperor* tell us much about the syncretic political thought known as "Huang-Lao" that was in vogue in early

Han times. The Yellow Emperor texts present a view of good government which combines practical Confucian and Legalist principles with Taoist metaphysics and psychology.

In two important cases the manuscripts found at Ma-wang-tui provide us with what are now the earliest known versions of well-known Chinese philosophical classics. One of these is the *I Ching (The Book of Changes)*, for which we find here the basic text for the sixty-four hexagrams and five different commentaries only one of which was previously known, the *Hsi-tz'u*, or "Appended Judgments" (the others are called *Erh-san-tzu wen* ["The Questions of the Disciples"], *Mou Ho*, *Chao Li*, and *Yao*).

The other case is the *Lao-tzu*: two copies of the *Lao-tzu* were found at Ma-wang-tui. Before this, the three earliest editions of the *Lao-tzu* were those associated with the commentaries of Yen Tsun (fl. 53–24 B.C.), Wang Pi (A.D. 226–249), and Ho-shang Kung (traditionally dated to the reign of Emperor Wen of the Han [179–157 B.C.], but dated by many to the third or fourth century A.D.). But all present versions of these three editions are "received" texts, having been copied many times over the centuries and thus passed down to the present. Our copies of these "early" texts, therefore, undoubtedly do not represent the text as it was seen by the commentators whose names they bear.[4] The need for a new translation of the *Lao-tzu* based on the Ma-wang-tui texts is thus very clear.[5]

II. THE MA-WANG-TUI MANUSCRIPTS OF THE *LAO-TZU* AND OTHER VERSIONS OF THE TEXT

The two *Lao-tzu* manuscripts, which we simply call Text A *(chia)* and Text B *(i)*, are not exactly the same, either in content or in style, sure evidence that even at this early date there was more than one version of the *Lao-tzu* in circulation. Differences in content will be noted in Part Two, "Text, Commentary, and Notes," below chapter by chapter. In terms of differences in style, the characters in Text A are written in "small seal" *(hsiao-chuan)* form, an old style of writing that was to be abandoned in the Han; the characters in Text B, by way of contrast, are written in the more modern "clerical" *(li)* script. This is one indication that Text A was copied before Text B. Further evidence proving this point is the fact that Text A does not avoid the taboo on the personal name of the founding emperor of the Han, Liu Pang (r. 206–194 B.C.) while Text B does, changing all *pang*'s ("country" or "state") in the text to *kuo*'s (also "country" or "state"). Text B, on the other hand, does not avoid using the taboo names of Emperors Hui (r. 194–187 B.C.) and Wen (r. 179–156 B.C.), Liu Ying, and Liu Heng, while later texts all change *ying* ("full") to *man* (also "full") and *heng* ("constant") to *ch'ang* (also "constant"). This seems to show that Text A was copied sometime before the reign of Liu Pang, while Text B was copied during it.[6]

In comparing the Ma-wang-tui texts of the *Lao-tzu* to later editions, let us state clearly at the outset that the Ma-wang-tui texts do not differ in any *radical* way from later versions of the text. That is to say, there are no chapters in the Ma-wang-tui texts that are not found in later texts and vice versa, and there is nothing in the Ma-wang-tui texts that would lead us to understand the philosophy of the text in a radically new way. The differences tend to be more subtle. A different word is used here and there, or a word, phrase, or line is added in or left out, or the syntax of a phrase or line is not the same. One of the striking features of the Ma-wang-tui texts of *Lao-tzu* in fact is that they are much more "grammatical" than later editions, using many more grammatical particles than later editions, but for that very reason being grammatically much more precise.

The word, phrase, and line variants in the Ma-wang-tui texts are pointed out below in Part Two chapter by chapter. Here in this introduction we want to note three other interesting ways in which the Ma-wang-tui texts are different from later ones, all having to do with overall form.

The standard texts of *Lao-tzu* are divided into two parts, chapters 1 through 37, which are sometimes called the *Tao* ("the Way"), and chapters 38 through 81, sometimes called the *Te* ("Virtue"). The Ma-wang-tui texts *do* have the same two-part division, but in reverse order: the "Virtue" part preceding "the Way." The two halves are labeled *Te* and *Tao*, and that is the only indication of a title for the book in the Ma-wang-tui texts.[7] In the Ma-wang-tui texts (both A and B), the book begins with what most texts call chapter 38 and ends with 37.

We still do not know why this was done. Some

scholars feel the Ma-wang-tui texts reflect the original order of the *Tao-te ching* and show that Lao-tzu (or the author) was all along more interested in social-political matters than he was in metaphysics and psychology, since the "Virtue" *(Te)* section has many chapters related to good government while "the Way" *(Tao)* has important chapters on the nature of the Way.* Kao Heng and Ch'ih Hsi-chao, on the other hand, pointing out that the order of the chapters in the Ma-wang-tui manuscripts agrees with the order found in the "Explaining *Lao-tzu*" chapter of the pre-Han Legalist text *Han-fei-tzu*, hypothesize that there were two different versions of the *Lao-tzu* in circulation in the early second century B.C., one with "the Way" *(Tao)* followed by "Virtue" *(Te)* and one in the Ma-wang-tui form, the former used by the Taoists and the latter used in the Legalist tradition.[8] But Yen Ling-feng feels that the Ma-wang-tui form of the text is simply the result of packaging. He suggests that the Ma-wang-tui texts or their predecessors were copied from texts written on strips of bamboo that were tied together in bundles, one for part I of the text and one for part II. But when the copyist was finished, he put the part I bundle into a box first with part II on top of it; the next copyist opening the box would naturally begin with the bundle of slips on top, which would be the part II bundle.[9]

Secondly, with one possible exception, there are no chapter divisions in the Ma-wang-tui texts, no chapter numbers or names; the text in each case essentially

---

*But there are many important chapters on the Way in part II as well, and good chapters on governing in part I.

reads as one continuous whole (except for the division into the *Te* and *Tao* parts). The exception to this is an important one: in part II of Text A there are black dots between characters every so often (we might call them "periods"), many of these, but not all, occurring at the beginning of present chapters.[10]

This seems to indicate that at the time when the Ma-wang-tui texts were copied the chapter divisions in the *Lao-tzu* were not yet firmly determined. We must then ask when were the present eighty-one chapters determined? And why was the number set at eighty-one? And, if this number proves to be arbitrary, is it possible that present chapter divisions are not always made at the *right* places, that is, at places where there is a clear change in theme and/or style?

I think the evidence shows that the present eighty-one chapters were determined around 50 B.C. and that the number eighty-one indeed bears no relation to the intent of the author or compiler.[11] The number eighty-one is a "perfect" one in Yin/Yang speculations since nine is the fullness of Yang (Yang qualities are heat, energy, power, and life) and eighty-one is the product of two nines.[12] And, in the present text, a number of chapter divisions exist where there should be none (see, for example, chapters 17–19 and chapters 67–69, each of which should be one continuous unit of text). By contrast, in a number of places two or more originally separate units of text now form a single chapter (chapter 29 is one such possibility).

Finally, were the Ma-wang-tui texts of *Lao-tzu* to be divided into chapters where the present-day text is divided, the sequence of material in the texts would be much the same. But there are three exceptions: what to us is chapter 24 comes between chapters 21 and 22 in the Ma-wang-tui texts; what to us is chapter 40 comes between chapters 41 and 42; what in present texts of the *Lao-tzu* are chapters 80 and 81 are placed between chapters 66 and 67 in the Ma-wang-tui texts. In the first two cases the Ma-wang-tui order seems to make sense in terms of the flow of ideas; why chapters 80 and 81 are placed where they are in the Ma-wang-tui texts remains unclear.

III. THE PHILOSOPHY OF LAO-TZU

A. *The Tao*

The starting point for understanding the philosophy of Lao-tzu is understanding what he means by the Tao, or the Way. The Way is Lao-tzu's name for ultimate reality (though he continually points out that he does not know its *true* name, he simply "calls" it the Way [for example, chapter 25]).[13] For Lao-tzu the Way is that reality, or that level of reality, that existed prior to and gave rise to all other things, the physical universe (Heaven and Earth), and all things in it, what the Chinese call the "ten thousand things" *(wan-wu)*.* The

---

*The "ten thousand things" is a collective designation in Chinese for the various genera and species of living things—the varieties of plants, animals, insects, and so forth (though on occasion the term might refer to inorganic phenomena as well). Man is simply one of the ten thousand things. Note that "Heaven and Earth" are not clearly indicated as coming from the Tao in line 3 in chapter 1 of the Ma-wang-tui texts of *Lao-tzu* (as they are in other versions of the text). Nonetheless, that "Heaven and Earth" come from the Tao is still clearly noted in chapters 6 and 25.

Way in a sense is like a great womb: it is empty and devoid in itself of differentiation, one in essence; yet somehow it contains all things in seedlike or embryo form, and all things "emerge" from the Tao in creation as babies emerge from their mothers (chapters 6 and 21).

But the Way does not simply give birth to all things. Having done so, it continues in some way to be present in each individual thing as an energy or power, a power that is not static but constantly on the move, inwardly pushing each thing to develop and grow in a certain way, in a way that is in accord with its true nature. The Way *in* things is generally what Taoists mean by *te*, "virtue." But note that Lao-tzu uses "virtue" in his text in two different ways. On occasion it means this life-energy in things (for example, at the start of chapter 55); but in other places (for example, chapter 38) it seems to mean virtue in the sense of morality, the sense in which it is used by the Confucians.

That the Tao is a feminine reality and a maternal reality thus seems clear. It is not surprising, therefore, that Lao-tzu refers to the Tao as the "Mother" in no less than five places—in chapters 1, 20, 25, 52, and 59.

Key chapters in the text on the nature of the Tao are chapters 1, 6, 14, 16, 21, 25, 34, and 52. The selfless "mothering" of the Tao is best described in chapter 34 of the text, which reads somewhat differently in its standard and Ma-wang-tui forms. Wing-tsit Chan's translation of the standard text reads:

1   The Great Tao flows everywhere. It may go left or right.
2   All things depend on it for life, and it does not turn away from them.

3 It accomplishes its task, but does not claim credit for it.
4 It clothes and feeds all things but does not claim to be master over them.
5 Always without desires, it may be called The Small.
6 All things come to it and it does not master them; it may be called The Great.
7 Therefore (the sage) never strives himself for the great, and thereby the great is achieved.[14]

In the Ma-wang-tui version of this chapter, lines 3 and 4 are quite different, and that the phrase "always without desires" in line 5 is out of place seems clear, in that without it lines 4 and 6 are strictly parallel to lines 7 and 8 (thus, it is the very thing that makes the Tao small that makes it great). The Ma-wang-tui version reads:

1 The Way floats and drifts;
2 It can go left or right.
3 It accomplishes its tasks and completes its affairs, and yet for this it is not given a name.*
4 The ten thousand things entrust their lives to it, and yet it does not act as their master.
5 Thus it is constantly without desires.
6 It can be named with the things that are small.
7 The ten thousand things entrust their lives to it, and yet it does not act as their master.

*To "have a name" (yu-ming) in classical Chinese means as well "to be famous." Thus we would expect anything that accomplishes its tasks and completes its affairs to be famous and well known, and yet that is not true for the Tao.

8 It can be named with the things that are great
9 Therefore the Sage's ability to accomplish the great
10 Comes from his not playing the role of the great.
11 Therefore he is able to accomplish the great.

There is an analogy that works well in helping us see exactly what kind of thing the Tao is and how it works. In that analogy the Tao resembles an untended and uncared-for ("uncultivated") field, and the varieties of wildflowers that grow in such a field represent the ten thousand things.[15] Were you to go to such a field in the winter, you would see only brown soil or white snow. The field appears to be one in essence, undifferentiated, and "empty" of all forms of life. Nonetheless, should you return to that field in May or June, you would discover that a marvelous transformation had occurred, the field now being filled with all kinds of wildflowers. There are, as it were, "ten thousand" different varieties of flowers, with each species (dandelion, nightshade, chickory, etc.) and each individual in each of the species being somehow unique in color and shape. And you now know that what had appeared to be devoid of life in the winter was in fact a very fecund womb, containing within itself in its oneness the seeds and roots of all different things.

Moreover, the work of the field does not end with springtime creation. For the field continues throughout the summer to care for and nourish each of its "children," supplying them with the water and nutriments that are vital for life. And in this nurturing work, the field cares for all of the flowers without discrimination, and it takes no credit for all that it does. The brown soil is always in the background and "unseen," our eyes being dazzled by the colors and forms of the flowers. Finally, the field accomplishes all that it does "without taking any action" *(wu-wei)*; that is to say, we never see the soil actively doing anything; all that happens seems to happen on its own "by nature." One of the things said about the Tao in the *Lao-tzu* a number of times is that it "does nothing, and yet there is nothing left undone" *(wu-wei erh wu-pu-wei)*.[16] And the ideal ruler in the *Lao-tzu* is someone who rules in this way. As the Tao is to the ten thousand things the ruler is to his people. The ideal ruler works to make it possible that all of his people will grow to maturity in good health and will feel free to be who or what by nature they are, yet he claims no credit for all that he does. As is said of the ideal ruler at the end of chapter 17: "He completes his tasks and finishes his affairs, Yet the common people say, 'these things all happened by nature.' "[17]

B. *Returning to the Way*

One of the things that seems to follow from the analogy of the Tao and the field is that for any individual flower (a) to be what it can be—for a sunflower to realize its "sunflowerness," its genetic makeup; and (b) to live out its natural lifespan (which varies with wildflowers from species to species), there is only one requirement that must be met—it must keep its roots firmly planted in the soil.

But this is precisely what humans do not do. That is to say, Lao-tzu seems to assume that something happens to people as individuals (and to societies as a whole) as they grow up such that as adults they are "uprooted" and have lost touch with the Way. As a result, adults constantly lose sight of who they are by nature and are constantly striving to be someone or something they are not, and they do things that lead them to physical danger and harm.[18] Consequently, if human beings are to be what they are, and what they can be, and live out their natural years free from harm, they must as adults *return* to the Way.

But what exactly does it mean to "return to the Way"? And how does one make that return?

These questions are not easy to answer, and here we can simply touch upon a few themes that seem relevant in the *Lao-tzu*. One thing to which Lao-tzu would have people return seems to be a simpler way of life, perhaps one lived with fewer possessions. Lao-tzu and the Taoists clearly recognize that possessions can easily end up "possessing" and that the more one has, the more one has to worry about. As he says in chapter 22, "When you have little, you'll attain [much]; With much, you'll be confused." The ideal in Taoist terms is to *chih-tsu*—"know contentment," or more literally "know when you have enough." And clearly the Taoists feel people really *need* a lot less than they think they do in terms of possessions and accomplishments to live healthy, happy, fulfilled lives.

Chapter 80 of the *Lao-tzu* could be understood as suggesting a social ideal in which the state would be composed of small farming communities, with very little, if any, central authority in the state, and in each village the people would be so content with their lives that even if they knew there were other villages nearby, they would have no desire to visit them. This chapter reads:

1 Let the country be small and people few—
2 Bring it about that there are weapons for "tens" and "hundreds," yet let no one use them;
3 Have the people regard death gravely and put migrating far from their minds.*
4 Though they might have boats and carriages, no one will ride them;
5 Though they might have armor and spears, no one will display them.
6 Have the people return to knotting cords and using them.
7 They will relish their food,
8 Regard their clothing as beautiful,
9 Delight in their customs,
10 And feel safe and secure in their homes.
11 Neighboring states might overlook one another,
12 And the sounds of chickens and dogs might be overheard,
13 Yet the people will arrive at old age and death with no comings and goings between them.

If this represents Lao-tzu's social ideal, then it is an ideal he shared with the "Agriculturalists" or "Tillers" (*nung-chia*) of the age, as Angus Graham has aptly shown.[19]

---

*This line is slightly different in the Ma-wang-tui texts than in the standard text. See the "Comments and Notes" on chapter 80, page 162.

A second way in which we can understand "return" in the philosophy of Lao-tzu is that he thought the Taoist must literally return to the Tao by achieving mystical union with the Tao—experiencing the oneness of all things in the Tao—and that some form of meditation would lead to this goal. The importance of meditation in early Taoism and the role it played in Taoist experience are points about which scholars disagree.[20] Would Lao-tzu have insisted that the *only* way to return to the Tao is by means of meditation and mystical experience? Did he and other Taoists have definite techniques that they followed in meditation? Answers to these kinds of questions do not come easy. The most we can say is that *if* Lao-tzu and his like practiced and advocated certain types of meditation, for some reason he chose not to elaborate on these techniques in his book.

Nonetheless, there certainly are places in the text that seem to allude to and possibly describe meditation and mystical insight, the key chapters and passages in this regard being lines 2–8 in chapter 56, lines 5–6 in chapter 1, and the beginning sections of chapters 10 and 16.

The opening lines of chapter 16 seem to lay out what must be done with the mind and the senses in meditation and then describe what can be seen by the adept with the mind emptied and the body stilled—the Taoist has insight into the true nature of things, seeing that all things come from and return to the Tao.[21]

1   Take emptiness to the limit;
2   Maintain tranquility in the center.

3   The ten thousand things—side-by-side they arise;
4   And by this I see their return.
5   Things [come forth] in great numbers;
6   Each one returns to its root.

Emptying the mind of all thoughts and perceptions so that the mind can be filled with new insight is not only commonly done in meditation, it seems to be something that Chuang-tzu advocated as well. In chapter 4 of the work that bears his name we find a description of the process of "mind fasting" *(hsin-chai)*, which goes: "Make your will one! Don't listen with your ears, listen with your mind. No, don't listen with your mind, but listen with your spirit. Listening stops with the ears, the mind stops with recognition, but spirit is empty and waits on all things. The Way gathers in emptiness alone. Emptiness is the fasting of the mind."[22] It is also of interest that the word in line 4 above that I translate as "see" is *kuan*, and *kuan* in Chinese has this sense of seeing into the true nature of something, having an insight. With the development of Buddhism later in China it was this *kuan* that was chosen to translate *vipaśyanā*, the "insight" that follows upon the "stopping" *(śamatha; chih* in Chinese) of the mind's normal functions.[23]

The intent of the opening lines of chapter 10 is more difficult to sort out. The lines in question are these:

1   In nourishing the soul and embracing the One—can you do it without letting them leave?

2 In concentrating your breath and making it soft—can
   you [make it like that of] a child?
3 In cultivating and cleaning your profound mirror—can
   you do it so that it has no blemish?

That the mind is like a bright-shining mirror that
must be wiped clean of all false thoughts and passions
(by concentration and mental effort) so that it can reflect things as they really are—such notions are inte-
gral to certain types of meditation and closely resemble
ideas attributed to Shen-hsiu, the founder of the
Northern School of Ch'an (Zen) Buddhism at the turn
of the eighth century in China.[24] But while line 3
might show us that early Taoists did indeed practice
some kind of insight meditation, lines 1 and 2 probably allude to Taoist longevity techniques. It is difficult
not to read later Taoist notions into the text at this
point. For one important type of meditation in later
Taoism is known as *shou-i*, "maintaining the one" or
"maintaining the three ones" (though our phrase here
is *pao-i*, "embrace the one"), where the Taoist was to
visualize three supreme deities in the three "fields of
cinnabar" in the body to *keep* them inside the body: if
they leave, the practitioner dies.[25] And there are many
types of meditation in later Taoism that have as their
goal passing pure breath *(ch'i)* through the body, in
this way making the flesh light, and learning to breathe
again like an infant, since baby's breath is unstained by
the world and still full of life.[26] Thus the breathing
practices and concentration alluded to here in lines 1
and 2 of chapter 10 are not so much the means to an

end (mystical insight) as they are the end in itself. They maintain the health and long life of the body.

Finally on the notion of "return" it seems clear that Lao-tzu wants people as adults to return to some things they all possessed more fully as children—namely genuineness, sincerity, and spontaneity. Such "natural" qualities are destroyed in a sense by education and acculturation. As children grow up, they "learn" from their parents and from others in society that some things and some types of behavior are "good" while others are "bad," some things are "beautiful" while others are "ugly," and some things are of "value" while others are not. But the appropriation of such sets of values, and the conscious striving to be "good" and not "bad" (of which Confucians approve) do not lead in the end, feel the Taoists, to "good" people and to peace and order in society. They lead rather to wrangling and disagreement (about what is right and what is wrong) and competition, to self-dissatisfaction, and to hypocrisy as people "act" in ways that they think others will approve of and value, rather than saying and doing what they genuinely feel. The important Taoist term *wu-wei* ("nonaction," literally "without action") in one sense *stands* for spontaneity and genuineness: it does not mean literally to do nothing, but rather "to act *without acting*," to spontaneously say and do what is genuinely felt rather than putting on a show for others ("acting").[27]

Thus, at the start of chapter 38 Lao-tzu notes that the truly virtuous person is the one who does the good thing spontaneously, unaware of and unconcerned with the fact that this is what others approve of as "virtue."

He says, "The highest virtue is not virtuous; therefore it truly has virtue. The lowest virtue never loses sight of its virtue; therefore it has no true virtue." And in chapter 19, having noted in chapter 18 that people are aware of the Confucian virtues of humanity *(jen)* and righteousness *(i)* only after the Great Tao declines, and that the advocacy of knowledge and wisdom simply leads to hypocrisy, Lao-tzu urges people to "Eliminate sageliness, throw away knowledge; And the people will benefit a hundredfold," and "Eliminate humanity, throw away righteousness; And the people will return to filial piety and compassion."[28] Lao-tzu and Chuang-tzu both talk as though there were a time in the beginning when everyone lived in accord with the Way and no distinctions were made between right and wrong. The Confucian advocacy of certain values—humanity, righteousness, filial piety *(hsiao)*, loyalty *(chung)*, and propriety *(li)*—was either the result of or the *cause* of a decline in the Way.[29]

C. Health, Long Life, and Immortality

In a number of places in the text, Lao-tzu makes the claim that the Taoist is "free from danger" or "free from harm" throughout his lifetime. In chapter 16 this is said of one who is one with the Tao; in chapters 32 and 44 it is said of one who knows to "stop in time"; and in chapter 52 it is said of one who understands the children (of the Tao) yet clings to the Mother.

The "danger" or "harm" alluded to here need not be understood in a literal, physical way. One could argue that one who knows the Tao and is content remains safe and secure no matter what happens to his or her body. But the word that is used here for danger—*tai*—tends to mean physical danger, and given all that Lao-tzu tells us of the sage in his text, it makes good sense that such a person would not suffer harm in a physical way. The Taoist sage is someone who puts himself in the background and does not compete; hence he will presumably have fewer enemies than one who aggressively strives for wealth and fame. Moreover we are told that the Taoist sage values calmness and tranquility and "has few desires" or "lessens his desires." He would seem to avoid, therefore, the anxieties and emotions that physically waste others away.

Moreover, it is evident that life itself is a value in Taoism: To live out one's natural years in peace, contentment, and tranquility is the goal. And Lao-tzu asks at the start of chapter 44, "Fame or your body—which is more dear? Your body or possessions—which is worth more? " Clearly Lao-tzu sees that in some cases a choice must be made between wealth and fame and one's life.[30] But we must hasten to add that Lao-tzu would also say, paradoxically, that it is precisely the person who is unconcerned, in a way, with matters of life and death who stands the best chance of living out his natural years. Obsessive clinging to life at all costs makes people vulnerable. As he says at the beginning of chapter 50, the reason many people move toward death in their actions is "because they regard life as LIFE."[31]

The second part of chapter 50 has sometimes been understood as showing that Taoists remain free from harm because they are somehow physically invulnerable; their bodies cannot be harmed. Those lines read:

7 You've no doubt heard of those who are good at holding on to life:
8 When walking through hills, they don't avoid rhinos and tigers;
9 When they go into battle, they don't put on armor or shields;
10 The rhino has no place to probe with its horn;
11 The tiger finds no place to put its claws.
12 And weapons find no place to hold their blades.
13 Now, why is this so?
14 Because there is no place for death in them.

While "no place for death in them" might later mean that the physical stuff of the Taoist has changed and is now matter that cannot be damaged or harmed, it is more likely that Lao-tzu means by these words that the one who is "good at holding on to life" is the one who is *unconcerned* about death (and in *this* way has "no place for death in him"), since he identifies with and values the Tao, that reality that transcends life and death.

These thoughts bring us to the issue of immortality in the thought of Lao-tzu. While it seems clear that health and long life—living out one's natural years—are two of the benefits enjoyed by the Taoist, is there more? Is there a notion of immortality here? Later in the Taoist religion, immortality is understood as a physical immortality: one normally becomes an immortal *(hsien)* through a process of "transubstantia-tion" in which one changes the substance of his or her body from gross, heavy, easily decaying matter into matter that is light, pure, and refined and capable of lasting a long time if not forever. There seems to be little in the *Lao-tzu* to support such later views unless we understand things said in chapters 50 and 55 in this way.

But are there indications of some kind of "spirit-ual" immortality for the Taoist? Lao-tzu says nothing straightforwardly and unambiguously about immortal-ity of any kind, nor does Chuang-tzu. Chuang-tzu in fact repeatedly tells us that we cannot know what lies beyond death; we can only "know" the state or condi-tion we are in at present.[32]

The issue of immortality in the *Lao-tzu* can be approached in two different ways—theoretically and textually. Theoretically we could certainly argue that insofar as the Tao is that one reality that existed before all other things and is an eternally existing reality, and insofar as the Taoist in some way becomes one with the Tao during his or her lifetime, that at death the Taoist realizes this oneness in the fullest possible way and en-joys the immortality of the Tao. This is an argument that would see Taoist mysticism as parallel in a sense to the Indian mysticism of the *Upanishads* and the *Bhagavad-gita*.

One could also argue in theory, however, that inso-far as the Tao is not only the one reality that existed before all other things but is also in some way identi-fied with the continuous process of change in the uni-verse of things, and insofar as the Taoist is in some way one with this Tao, then at death his matter and energies are reabsorbed into the cosmic storehouse of matter and energy that is the Tao, to be reused later on in producing new things. This is a view that finds support in the *Chuang-tzu*, where one of his characters addresses a friend who is about to die with the words, "How marvelous the Creator [= the Tao] is! What is he going to make of you next? Where is he going to send you? Will he make you into a rat's liver? Will he make you into a bug's arm?"[33] This may or may not be a type of immortality that people find appealing;[34] nonetheless it is a *kind* of immortality.

Three passages in the text are relevant to the immortality issue. First of all, in the standard text of *Lao-tzu* (but not in the Ma-wang-tui texts) at the end of chapter 16 we are told that someone who is one with the Tao is "everlasting," and in chapters 44 and 59 the Taoist is said to be someone who "long endures." For some readers these words imply a kind of immortality.[35] But the words themselves *(chiu* in the first case, *ch'ang-chiu* in the second) literally mean no more than lasts "a long time" and "a very long time."

Secondly, in chapters 16 and 52 we find the words *mo-shen pu-tai*, which literally mean "end-life no-harm," and these are the words that are often translated as "to the end of his days he suffers no harm." However, these four characters can *also* mean "lose-body not-end," and they could be read as saying, therefore, that even though the Taoist at death loses his body, he does not come to *a total and final end*. Arthur Waley reads these characters in this way at the end of chapter 16, where he translates: "Tao is forever and he that possesses it, Though his body ceases, is not destroyed."[36]

Finally, at the end of chapter 33 of the *Lao-tzu*, we find the line *ssu-erh-pu-wang-che shou*, which Wing-tsit Chan translates as "He who dies but does not really perish enjoys long life." Clearly the question here is what does Lao-tzu mean by "perish"? And one of the things "perish" can mean is to be "totally wiped out" and "destroyed." Thus this line really could say that *true* long life is to continue on in some way after death, since one is not totally destroyed. But the word "perish" *(wang)* is also often understood to mean "to come to an unnatural end," to die before one's time, in which case this says nothing about immortality. D. C. Lau understands the line in this way, translating, "He who lives out his days has had a long life."[37]

Importantly, the Ma-wang-tui texts of the *Lao-tzu* do not have this *wang* ("to perish") in the text but rather the *wang* that means "to forget." They would appear to say, therefore, "To die but not be forgotten—that's true long life."

PART ONE

TRANSLATION

TRANSLATOR'S NOTE

Because readers of the *Te-tao ching* fall into two groups with different levels of expertise, I have repeated the translation in two independent segments.

Part One, "The Translation," is a straightforward presentation of the entire text with the corrections and emendations noted in Part Two. It is intended for the general reader.

Part Two, "Text, Commentary, and Notes," is aimed at the specialist reader, and repeats the translation. However, it is accompanied by notes which indicate the differences between Text A and Text B, discuss how each line of texts A and B differs from the received text, and add anything else which seems relevant to an understanding of the Ma-wang-tui silk manuscripts. For readers of Chinese, Part Two also includes corrected Chinese transcriptions of Text A and Text B.

The translation which appears in both Part One and Part Two is primarily a translation of Text B of the Ma-wang-tui texts: the Text A version of a chapter is used in seventeen cases —for chapters 1, 31, 42, 43, 44, 45, 46, 50, 51, 52, 56, 61, 62, 63, 69, 76, and 79. In those cases, what remains of Text A—the older of the two manuscripts—is more complete, and therefore more readily translated, than what remains of Text B.

The sequence of the translation is the sequence we find in the Ma-wang-tui texts. However, to facilitate reading and comparison, chapter divisions are made, and chapter numbers indicated, where they occur in modern texts. Chapter numbers are in brackets, to remind the reader that these numbers are not found in the original.

T E

(VIRTUE)

[CHAPTER 38]

The highest virtue is not virtuous; therefore it truly
  has virtue.
The lowest virtue never loses sight of its virtue;
  therefore it has no true virtue.

The highest virtue takes no action, yet it has no reason
  for acting this way;
The highest humanity takes action, yet it has no
  reason for acting this way;
The highest righteousness takes action, and it has its
  reasons for acting this way;
The highest propriety takes action, and when no one
  responds to it, then it angrily rolls up its sleeves
  and forces people to comply.

Therefore, when the Way is lost, only then do we have
  virtue;
When virtue is lost, only then do we have humanity;
When humanity is lost, only then do we have
  righteousness;
And when righteousness is lost, only then do we have
  propriety.

As for propriety, it's but the thin edge of loyalty and
  sincerity, and the beginning of disorder.
And foreknowledge is but the flower of the Way, and
  the beginning of stupidity.

Therefore the Great Man
Dwells in the thick and doesn't dwell in the thin;
Dwells in the fruit and doesn't dwell in the flower.
Therefore, he rejects that and takes this.

[CHAPTER 39]

Of those in the past that attained the One—
Heaven, by attaining the One became clear;
Earth, by attaining the One became stable;
Gods, by attaining the One became divine;
Valleys, by attaining the One became full;
Marquises and kings, by attaining the One made the
    whole land ordered and secure.

Taking this to its logical conclusion we would say—
If Heaven were not by means of it clear, it would, I'm
    afraid, shatter;
If the Earth were not by means of it stable, it would,
    I'm afraid, let go.
If the gods were not by means of it divine, they would,
    I'm afraid, be powerless.
If valleys were not by means of it full, they would, I'm
    afraid, dry up.
And if marquises and kings were not by means of it
    noble and high, they would, I'm afraid, topple and
    fall.

Therefore, it must be the case that the noble has the
    base as its root;
And it must be the case that the high has the low for
    its foundation.
Thus, for this reason, marquises and kings call
    themselves "The Orphan," "The Widower," and
    "The One Without Grain."
This is taking the base as one's root, is it not?!

Therefore, they regard their large numbers of carriages
    as having no carriage.
And because of this, they desire not to dazzle and
    glitter like jade,
But to remain firm and strong like stone.

[CHAPTER 41]

When the highest type of men hear the Way, with
    diligence they're able to practice it;
When average men hear the Way, some things they
    retain and others they lose;
When the lowest type of men hear the Way, they laugh
    out loud at it.
If they didn't laugh at it, it couldn't be regarded as the
    Way.

Therefore, there is a set saying about this that goes:
The bright Way appears to be dark;
The Way that goes forward appears to retreat;
The smooth Way appears to be uneven;
The highest virtue is empty like a valley;
The purest white appears to be soiled;
Vast virtue appears to be insufficient;
Firm virtue appears thin and weak;
The simplest reality appears to change.

The Great Square has no corners;
The Great Vessel takes long to complete;
The Great Tone makes little sound;
The Great Image has no shape.

The Way is Great but has no name.
Only the Way is good at beginning things and also
    good at bringing things to completion.

[CHAPTER 40]

"Reversal" is the movement of the Tao;
"Weakness" is the function of the Tao.

The things of the world originate in being,
And being originates in nonbeing.

[CHAPTER 42]

The Way gave birth to the One;
The One gave birth to the Two;
The Two gave birth to the Three;
And the Three gave birth to the ten thousand things.
The ten thousand things carry Yin on their backs and
    wrap their arms around Yang.
Through the blending of ch'i they arrive at a state of
    harmony.

The things that are hated by the whole world
Are to be orphaned, widowed, and have no grain.
Yet kings and dukes take these as their names.
Thus with all things—some are increased by taking
    away;
While some are diminished by adding on.

Therefore, what other men teach,
I will also consider and then teach to others.
Thus, "The strong and violent do not come to a
    natural end."
I will take this as the father of my studies.

[CHAPTER 43]

The softest, most pliable thing in the world runs
    roughshod over the firmest thing in the world.
That which has no substance gets into that which has
    nc spaces or cracks.
I therefore know that there is benefit in taking no
    action.
The wordless teaching, the benefit of taking no
    action—
Few in the world can realize these!

[CHAPTER 44]

Fame or your health—which is more dear?
Your health or possessions—which is worth more?
Gain or loss—in which is there harm?
If your desires are great, you're bound to be
    extravagant;
If you store much away, you're bound to lose a great
    deal.
Therefore, if you know contentment, you'll not be
    disgraced.
If you know when to stop, you'll suffer no harm.
And in this way you can last a very long time.

[CHAPTER 45]

Great completion seems incomplete;
Yet its usefulness is never exhausted.
Great fullness seems to be empty;
Yet its usefulness is never used up.
Great straightness seems to be bent.
Great skill seems to be clumsy.
Great eloquence seems to stammer;
Great surplus seems to be lacking.
Activity overcomes cold;
Tranquility overcomes heat.
If you're quiet and tranquil you can become the ruler
    of the world.

[CHAPTER 46]

When the world has the Way, ambling horses are
    retired to fertilize fields.
When the world lacks the Way, war horses are reared
    in the suburbs.

Of crimes—none is greater than having things that one
    desires;
Of disasters—none is greater than not knowing when
    one has enough.
Of defects—none brings more sorrow than the desire
    to attain.
Therefore, the contentment one has when he knows
    that he has enough, is abiding contentment indeed.

[CHAPTER 47]

No need to leave your door to know the whole world;
No need to peer through your windows to know the
    Way of Heaven.
The farther you go, the less you know.

Therefore the Sage knows without going,
Names without seeing,
And completes without doing a thing.

[CHAPTER 48]

Those who work at their studies increase day after day;
Those who have heard the Tao decrease day after day.
They decrease and decrease till they get to the point
   where they do nothing.
They do nothing and yet there's nothing left undone.
When someone wants to take control of the world, he
   must always be unconcerned with affairs.
For in a case where he's concerned with affairs,
He'll be unworthy, as well, of taking control of the
   world.

[CHAPTER 49]

The Sage constantly has no set mind;
He takes the mind of the common people as his mind.
Those who are good he regards as good;
Those who are not good he also regards as good.
In this way he attains goodness.
Those who are trustworthy he trusts;
And those who are not trustworthy he also trusts.
In this way he gets their trust.
As for the Sage's presence in the world—he is one
    with it.
And with the world he merges his mind.
The common people all fix their eyes and ears on him.
And the Sage treats them all as his children.

[CHAPTER 50]

We come out into life and go back into death.
The companions of life are thirteen;
The companions of death are thirteen;
And yet people, because they regard life as LIFE, in
    all of their actions move toward the thirteen that
    belong to the realm of death.
Now, why is this so?
It's because they regard life as LIFE.

You've no doubt heard of those who are good at
    holding on to life:
When walking through hills, they don't avoid rhinos
    and tigers;
When they go into battle, they don't put on armor or
    shields;
The rhino has no place to probe with its horn;
The tiger finds no place to put its claws.
And weapons find no place to hold their blades.
Now, why is this so?
Because there is no place for death in them.

[CHAPTER 51]

The Way gives birth to them and Virtue nourishes
    them;
Substance gives them form and their unique capacities
    complete them.
Therefore the ten thousand things venerate the Way
    and honor Virtue.
As for their veneration of the Way and their honoring
    of Virtue—
No one rewards them for it; it's constantly so on its
    own.

The Way gives birth to them, nourishes them, matures
    them, completes them, rests them, rears them,
    supports them, and protects them.
It gives birth to them but doesn't try to own them;
It acts on their behalf but doesn't make them
    dependent;
It matures them but doesn't rule them.
This we call Profound Virtue.

The world had a beginning,
Which can be considered the mother of the world.
Having attained the mother, in order to understand her
    children,
If you return and hold on to the mother, till the end of
    your life you'll suffer no harm.

Block up the holes;
Close the doors;
And till the end of your life you'll not labor.
Open the holes;
Meddle in affairs;
And till the end of your life you'll not be saved.

To perceive the small is called "discernment."
To hold on to the pliant is called "strength."
If you use the rays to return to the bright light,
You'll not abandon your life to peril.
This is called Following the Constant.

[CHAPTER 53]

Were I to have the least bit of knowledge, in walking
    on a Great Road, it's only going astray that I
    would fear.
The Great Way is very level;
But people greatly delight in tortuous paths.

The courts are swept very clean;
While the fields are full of weeds;
And the granaries are all empty.
Their clothing—richly embroidered and colored;
While at their waists they carry sharp swords.
They gorge themselves on food, and of possessions
    and goods they have plenty.

This is called thievery!
And thievery certainly isn't the Way!

[CHAPTER 54]

What is firmly set up can't be pulled down;
What is firmly embraced cannot slip free.
And your sons and grandsons, as a result, will sacrifice
    without end.

When you cultivate it in your person, your virtue will
    then be genuine;
When you cultivate it in your family, your virtue will
    then overflow;
When you cultivate it in your village, your virtue
    will then be long lasting;
When you cultivate it in your state, your virtue will
    then be abundant;
And when you cultivate it throughout the world, your
    virtue will then be widespread.

Use the individual to examine the individual;
Use the family to examine the family;
Use the village to examine the village;
Use the state to examine the state;
And use the world to examine the world;
How do I know that the world is so?
By this.

[CHAPTER 55]

One who embraces the fullness of Virtue,
Can be compared to a newborn babe.
Wasps and scorpions, snakes and vipers do not sting
    him;
Birds of prey and fierce beasts do not seize him;
His bones and muscles are weak and pliant, yet his
    grasp is firm;
He does not yet know the meeting of male and female,
    yet his organ is aroused—
This is because his essence is at its height.
He can scream all day, yet he won't become hoarse—
This is because his harmony is at its height.

To know harmony is called "the constant";
To know the constant is called "being wise";
To add on to life is called a "bad omen";
For the mind to control the breath—that's called
    "forcing things."

When things reach their prime, they get old;
This is called "not the Way."
What is not the Way will come to an early end.

[CHAPTER 56]

Those who know don't talk about it; those who talk
    don't know it.

He blocks up his holes,
Closes his doors,
Softens the glare,
Settles the dust,
Files down the sharp edges,
And unties the tangles.
This is called Profound Union.

Therefore, there is no way to get intimate with him,
But there is also no way to shun him.
There is no way to benefit him,
But there is also no way to harm him.
There is no way to ennoble him,
But there is also no way to debase him.
For this very reason he's the noblest thing in the
    world.

[CHAPTER 57]

Use the upright and correct to order the state;
Use surprise tactics when you use troops;
Use unconcern with affairs to take control of the
    world.

How do I know that this is so?
Well, the more taboos and prohibitions there are in the
    world, the poorer the people will be;
The more sharp weapons the people possess, the more
    muddled the states will be;
The more knowledge and skill people have, the more
    novel things will appear;
The more legal matters are made prominent, the more
    robbers and thieves there will be.

Therefore, the words of the Sage say:
I do nothing, and the people of themselves are
    transformed;
I love tranquility, and the people of themselves are
    upright;
I'm unconcerned with affairs, and the people of
    themselves become rich;
I desire not to desire, and the people of themselves are
    genuine and simple, like uncarved wood.

[CHAPTER 58]

When the government is muddled and confused,
The people are genuine and sincere.
When the government is discriminate and clear,
The state is crafty and cunning.

Disaster is that on which good fortune depends.
Good fortune is that in which disaster's concealed.
Who knows where it will end?
For there is no fixed "correct."
The "correct" turns into the "deviant";
And "good" turns into "evil."
People's state of confusion
Has certainly existed for a long time.
Therefore be square but don't cut;
Be sharp but don't stab;
Be straightforward but not unrestrained;
Be bright but don't dazzle.

[CHAPTER 59]

For ordering humanity and serving Heaven, nothing's
   so good as being sparing.
For only if you are sparing can you, therefore, early
   submit to the Way.
Early submission—this is called to repeatedly
   accumulate Virtue.
If you repeatedly accumulate Virtue, then there is
   nothing you can't overcome.
When there is nothing you can't overcome, no one
   knows where it will end.
When no one knows where it will end, you can possess
   the state.
And when you possess the mother of the state, you can
   last a very long time.
This is called having deep roots and a firm base,
It's the Way of long life and long-lasting vision.

[CHAPTER 60]

Ruling a large state is like cooking small fish.

When you use the Way to govern the world, evil
    spirits won't have godlike power.
Actually, it's not that evil spirits won't have godlike
    power,
It's that their power will not harm men.
But it's not just that *their* power won't harm men,
The Sage, also, will not harm them.
Since these two do not harm others,
Therefore their Virtues intermingle and return to
    them.

[CHAPTER 61]

The large state is like the lower part of a river;
It is the female of the world;
It is the meeting point of the world.
The female constantly overcomes the male with
    tranquility.
Because she is tranquil, therefore she is fittingly
    underneath.

The large state—if it is below the small state, then it
    takes over the small state;
The small state—if it is below the large state, then it
    is taken over *by* the large state.
Therefore some by being low take over,
And some by being low are taken over.

Therefore the large state merely desires to unite and
    rear others;
While the small state merely desires to enter and serve
    others.
If both get what they want,
Then the large state should fittingly be underneath.

[CHAPTER 62]

The Way is that toward which all things flow.
It is the treasure of the good man,
And that which protects the bad.

Beautiful words can be bought and sold;
Honored deeds can be presented to others as gifts;
Even with things that people regard as no good—will
    they be rejected?
Therefore, when the Son of Heaven is being enthroned
    or the Three Ministers installed,
Though you might salute them with disks of jade
    preceded by teams of four horses,
That's not so good as sitting still and offering this.
The reason why the ancients valued this—what was it?
Did they not say, "Those who seek, with this will
    attain, and those who commit offenses, with this
    will escape"?!
Therefore, it's the most valued thing in the world.

[CHAPTER 63]

Act without acting;
Serve without concern for affairs;
Find flavor in what has no flavor.

Regard the small as large and the few as many,
And repay resentment with kindness.
Plan for the difficult while it is easy;
Act on the large while it's minute.
The most difficult things in the world begin as things
    that are easy;
The largest things in the world arise from the minute.
Therefore the Sage, to the end does not strive to do the
    great,
And as a result, he is able to accomplish the great;
Those who too lightly agree will necessarily be trusted
    by few;
And those who regard many things as easy will
    necessarily end up with many difficulties.
Therefore, even the Sage regards things as difficult,
And as a result, in the end he has no difficulty.

[CHAPTER 64]

What is at rest is easy to hold;
What has not yet given a sign is easy to plan for;
The brittle is easily shattered;
The minute is easily scattered;
Act on it before it comes into being;
Order it before it turns into chaos.

A tree so big that it takes both arms to surround starts
    out as the tiniest shoot;
A nine-story terrace rises up from a basket of dirt.
A high place one hundred, one thousand feet high
    begins from under your feet.

Those who act on it ruin it;
Those who hold on to it lose it.
Therefore the Sage does not act,
And as a result, he doesn't ruin things;
He does not hold on to things,
And as a result, he doesn't lose things;
In people's handling of affairs, they always ruin things
    when they're right at the point of completion.
Therefore we say, "If you're as careful at the end as
    you were at the beginning, you'll have no failures."
Therefore the Sage desires not to desire and doesn't
    value goods that are hard to obtain;
He learns not to learn and returns to what the masses
    pass by;
He could help all things to be natural, yet he dare not
    do it.

[CHAPTER 65]

Those who practiced the Way in antiquity,
Did not use it to enlighten the people.
Rather, they used it to make them dumb.
Now the reason why people are difficult to rule is
    because of their knowledge;
As a result, to use knowledge to rule the state
Is thievery of the state;
To use ignorance to rule the state
Is kindness to the state.
One who constantly understands these two,
Also understands the principle.
To constantly understand the principle—
This is called Profound Virtue.
Profound Virtue is deep, is far-reaching,
And together with things it returns.
Thus we arrive at the Great Accord.

[CHAPTER 66]

The reason why rivers and oceans are able to be the
    kings of the one hundred valleys is that they are
    good at being below them.
For this reason they are able to be the kings of the one
    hundred valleys.

Therefore in the Sage's desire to be above the people,
He must in his speech be below them.
And in his desire to be at the front of the people,
He must in his person be behind them.
Thus he dwells above, yet the people do not regard
    him as heavy;
And he dwells in front, yet the people do not see him
    as posing a threat.
The whole world delights in his praise and never tires
    of him.
Is it not because he is not contentious,
That, as a result, no one in the world can contend with
    him?!

CHAPTER 80

Let the states be small and people few—
Bring it about that there are weapons for "tens" and
"hundreds," yet let no one use them;
Have the people regard death gravely and put
migrating far from their minds.
Though they might have boats and carriages, no one
will ride them;
Though they might have armor and spears, no one will
display them.
Have the people return to knotting cords and using
them.

They will relish their food,
Regard their clothing as beautiful,
Delight in their customs,
And feel safe and secure in their homes.
Neighboring states might overlook one another,
And the sounds of chickens and dogs might be
overheard,
Yet the people will arrive at old age and death with no
comings and goings between them.

[CHAPTER 81]

Sincere words are not showy;
Showy words are not sincere.
Those who know are not "widely learned";
Those "widely learned" do not know.
The good do not have a lot;
Those with a lot are not good.

The Sage accumulates nothing.
Having used what he had for others,
He has even more.
Having given what he had to others,
What he has is even greater.
Therefore, the Way of Heaven is to benefit and not
    cause any harm;
The Way of Man is to act on behalf of others and not
    to compete with them.

[CHAPTER 67]

Chapters 67, 68, and 69 should be read together as a unit.

The whole world says, I'm Great;
Great, yet unlike everyone else.
But it's precisely because I'm unlike everyone else, that
   I'm therefore able to be Great.
Were I like everyone else, for a long time now I'd have
   seemed insignificant and small.

I constantly have three treasures;
Hold on to them and treasure them.
The first is compassion;
The second is frugality;
And the third is not presuming to be at the forefront
   in the world.
Now, it's because I'm compassionate that I therefore
   can be courageous;
And it's because I'm frugal that I therefore can be
   magnanimous;
And it's because I don't presume to be at the forefront
   in the world that I therefore can be the head of
   those with complete talent.
Now, if you abandon this compassion and yet try to be
   courageous,
And if you abandon this frugality and yet try to be
   magnanimous,
And if you abandon this staying behind and yet go to
   the fore,
Then you will die.
If with compassion you attack, then you'll win;
If you defend, then you'll stand firm.

When Heaven's about to establish him,
It's as though he surrounds him with the protective
wall of compassion.

[CHAPTER 68]
Chapters 67, 68, and 69 should be read together as a unit.

Therefore, one who is good at being a warrior doesn't
    make a show of his might;
One who is good in battle doesn't get angry;
One who is good at defeating the enemy doesn't
    engage him.
And one who is good at using men places himself
    below them.
This is called the virtue of not competing;
This is called correctly using men;
This is called matching Heaven.
It's the high point of the past.

[CHAPTER 69]

Chapters 67, 68, and 69 should be read together as a unit.

Those who use weapons have a saying which goes:
"I don't presume to act like the host, and instead play
    the part of the guest;
I don't advance an inch, but rather retreat a foot."
This is called moving forward without moving
    forward—
Rolling up one's sleeves without baring one's arms—
Grasping firmly without holding a weapon—
And enticing to fight when there's no opponent.
Of disasters, none is greater than thinking you have no
    rival.
To think you have no rival is to come close to losing
    my treasures.
Therefore, when weapons are raised and the opponents
    are fairly well matched,
Then it's the one who feels grief that will win.

[CHAPTER 70]

My words are easy to understand,
And easy to put into practice.
Yet no one in the world can understand them,
And no one can put them into practice.
Now my words have an ancestor, and my deeds have
   a lord,
And it's simply because people have no understanding
   of *them*, that they therefore don't understand me.
But when those who understand me are few, then I'm
   of great value.
Therefore the Sage wears coarse woolen cloth, but
   inside it he holds on to jade.

[CHAPTER 71]

To know you don't know is best.
Not to know you don't know is a flaw.
Therefore, the Sage's not being flawed
Stems from his recognizing a flaw as a flaw.
Therefore, he is flawless.

[CHAPTER 72]

When the people don't respect those in power, then
    what they greatly fear is about to arrive.

Don't narrow the size of the places in which they live;
Don't oppress them in their means of livelihood.
It's simply because you do not oppress them, that they
    therefore will not be fed up.
Therefore the Sage knows himself but doesn't show
    himself;
He cherishes himself but doesn't value himself.
For this reason, he rejects that and takes this.

CHAPTER 73

If you're brave in being daring, you'll be killed;
If you're brave in not being daring, you'll live.
With these two things, in one case there's profit, in the
    other there's harm.
The things Heaven hates—who knows why?
The Way of Heaven is not to fight yet to be good at
    winning—
Not to speak yet skillfully respond—
No one summons it, yet it comes on its own—
To be at ease yet carefully plan.
Heaven's net is large and vast;
Its mesh may be coarse yet nothing slips through.

[CHAPTER 74]

If the people were constant in their behavior and yet
    did not fear death,
How could you use execution to intimidate them?
If you brought it about that the people were constant
    in their behavior and moreover feared death, and
    we took those who behaved in abnormal ways and
    killed them—who would dare act in this way?!
If the people are constant and moreover necessarily
    fear death, then we constantly have the one in
    charge of executions.
Now, killing people in place of the one in charge of
    executions, this is like cutting wood in place of the
    head carpenter.
And of those who cut wood in place of the head
    carpenter, very few do not hurt their hands!

CHAPTER 75

The reason why people starve,
Is because they take so much in tax-grain.
Therefore they starve.
The reason why the common people cannot be ruled,
Is because their superiors have their reasons for acting.
Therefore they cannot be ruled.

The reason why people take death lightly,
Is because they so avidly seek after life.
Therefore they take death lightly.
Only those who do not act for the purpose of living—
Only these are superior to those who value life.

When people are born, they're supple and soft;
When they die, they end up stretched out firm and
    rigid;
When the ten thousand things and grasses and trees
    are alive, they're supple and pliant;
When they're dead, they're withered and dried out.
Therefore we say that the firm and rigid are
    companions of death,
While the supple, the soft, the weak, and the delicate
    are companions of life.
If a soldier is rigid, he won't win;
If a tree is rigid, it will come to its end.
Rigidity and power occupy the inferior position;
Suppleness, softness, weakness, and delicateness
    occupy the superior position.

[CHAPTER 77]

The Way of Heaven is like the flexing of a bow.
The high it presses down; the low it raises up.
From those with a surplus it takes away; to those
   without enough it adds on.
Therefore the Way of Heaven—
Is to reduce the excessive and increase the insufficient;
The Way of Man—
Is to reduce the insufficient and offer more to the
   excessive.
Now, who is able to have a surplus and use it to offer
   to Heaven?
Clearly, it's only the one who possesses the Way.
Therefore the Sage—
Takes actions but does not possess them;
Accomplishes his tasks but does not dwell on them.
Like this, is his desire not to make a display of his
   worthiness.

[CHAPTER 78]

In the whole world, nothing is softer and weaker than
 water.
And yet for attacking the hard and strong, nothing can
 beat it,
Because there is nothing you can use to replace it.
That water can defeat the unyielding—
That the weak can defeat the strong—
There is no one in the whole world who doesn't
 know it,
And yet there is no one who can put it into practice.
For this reason, the words of the Sage say:
To take on yourself the disgrace of the state—this is
 called being the lord of the altars of earth and
 grain;
To assume responsibility for all ill-omened events in
 the state—this is called being the king of the
 world.
Correct words seem to say the reverse of what you
 expect them to say.

[CHAPTER 79]

To make peace where there has been great resentment,
   there is bound to be resentment left over.
How could this be regarded as good?
Therefore the Sage holds the right tally yet makes no
   demands of others.
For this reason, those who have virtue are in charge of
   the tally;
Those without virtue are in charge of the taxes.
The Way of Heaven has no favorites,
It's always with the good man.

Virtue—3,041 characters

TAO

(THE WAY)

[CHAPTER 1]

As for the Way, the Way that can be spoken of is not
the constant Way;
As for names, the name that can be named is not the
constant name.
The nameless is the beginning of the ten thousand
things;
The named is the mother of the ten thousand things.

Therefore, those constantly without desires, by this
means will perceive its subtlety.
Those constantly with desires, by this means will see
only that which they yearn for and seek.

These two together emerge;
They have different names yet they're called the same;
That which is even more profound than the
profound—
The gateway of all subtleties.

[CHAPTER 2]

When everyone in the world knows the beautiful as
 beautiful, ugliness comes into being;
When everyone knows the good, then the not good
 comes to be.
The mutual production of being and nonbeing,
The mutual completion of difficult and easy,
The mutual formation of long and short,
The mutual filling of high and low,
The mutual harmony of tone and voice,
The mutual following of front and back—
These are all constants.

Therefore the Sage dwells in nonactive affairs and
 practices the wordless teaching.
The ten thousand things arise, but he doesn't begin
 them;
He acts on their behalf, but he doesn't make them
 dependent;
He accomplishes his tasks, but he doesn't dwell on
 them;
It is only because he doesn't dwell on them that they
 therefore do not leave him.

[CHAPTER 3]

By not elevating the worthy, you bring it about that
people will not compete.
By not valuing goods that are hard to obtain, you
bring it about that people will not act like thieves.
By not displaying the desirable you bring it about that
people will not be confused.

Therefore, in the government of the Sage:
He empties their minds,
And fills their bellies.
Weakens their ambition,
And strengthens their bones.

He constantly causes the people to be without
knowledge and without desires.
If he can bring it about that those with knowledge
simply do not dare to act,
Then there is nothing that will not be in order.

[CHAPTER 4]

The Way is empty;
Yet when you use it, you never need fill it again.
Like an abyss! It seems to be the ancestor of the ten
    thousand things.

It files down sharp edges;
Unties the tangles;
Softens the glare;
And settles the dust.

Submerged! It seems perhaps to exist.
We don't know whose child it is;
It seems to have even preceded the Lord.

[CHAPTER 5]

Heaven and Earth are not humane;
They regard the ten thousand things as straw dogs.
The Sage is not humane;
He regards the common people as straw dogs.

The space between Heaven and Earth—is it not like a
    bellows?
It is empty and yet not depleted;
Move it and more always comes out.
Much learning means frequent exhaustion.
That's not so good as holding on to the mean.

[CHAPTER 6]

The valley spirit never dies;
We call it the mysterious female.
The gates of the mysterious female—
These we call the roots of Heaven and Earth.
Subtle yet everlasting! It seems to exist.
In being used, it is not exhausted.

[CHAPTER 7]

Heaven endures; Earth lasts a long time.
The reason why Heaven and Earth can endure and last
    a long time—
Is that they do not live for themselves.
Therefore they can long endure.

Therefore the Sage:
Puts himself in the background yet finds himself in the
    foreground;
Puts self-concern out of his mind, yet finds that his
    self-concern is preserved.
Is it not because he has no self-interest,
That he is therefore able to realize his self-interest?

[CHAPTER 8]

The highest good is like water;
Water is good at benefiting the ten thousand things
    and yet it does not compete with them.
It dwells in places the masses of people detest,
Therefore it is close to the Way.

In dwelling, the good thing is the land;
In the mind, the good thing is depth;
In giving, the good thing is being like Heaven;
In speaking, the good thing is sincerity;
In governing, the good thing is order;
In affairs, the good thing is ability;
In activity, the good thing is timeliness.

It is only because it does not compete, that therefore it
    is without fault.

[CHAPTER 9]

To hold it upright and fill it,
Is not so good as stopping in time.
When you pound it out and give it a point,
It won't be preserved very long.
When gold and jade fill your rooms,
You'll never be able to protect them.
Arrogance and pride with wealth and rank,
On their own bring on disaster.
When the deed is accomplished you retire;
Such is Heaven's Way!

[CHAPTER 10]

In nourishing the soul and embracing the One—can
   you do it without letting them leave?
In concentrating your breath and making it soft—can
   you make it like that of a child?
In cultivating and cleaning your profound mirror—
   can you do it so that it has no blemish?
In loving the people and giving life to the state—can
   you do it without using knowledge?
In opening and closing the gates of Heaven—can you
   play the part of the female?
In understanding all within the four reaches—can you
   do it without using knowledge?

Give birth to them and nourish them.
Give birth to them but don't try to own them;
Help them to grow but don't rule them.
This is called Profound Virtue.

[CHAPTER 11]

Thirty spokes unite in one hub;
It is precisely where there is nothing, that we find the
usefulness of the wheel.
We fire clay and make vessels;
It is precisely where there's no substance, that we find
the usefulness of clay pots.
We chisel out doors and windows;
It is precisely in these empty spaces, that we find the
usefulness of the room.
Therefore, we regard having something as beneficial;
But having nothing as useful.

[CHAPTER 12]

The five colors cause one's eyes to go blind.
Racing horses and hunting cause one's mind to go
mad.
Goods that are hard to obtain pose an obstacle to one's
travels.
The five flavors confuse one's palate.
The five tones cause one's ears to go deaf.

Therefore, in the government of the Sage:
He's for the belly and not for the eyes.
Thus he rejects that and takes this.

[CHAPTER 13]

"Regard favor and disgrace with alarm."
"Respect great distress as you do your own person."
What do I mean when I say "Regard favor and
    disgrace with alarm"?
Favor is inferior.
If you get it—be alarmed!
If you lose it—be alarmed!
This is what I mean when I say "Regard favor and
    disgrace with alarm."
What do I mean when I say "Respect great distress as
    you do your own person"?
The reason why I have great distress
Is that I have a body.
If I had no body, what distress would I have?
Therefore, to one who values acting for himself over
    acting on behalf of the world,
You can entrust the world.
And to one who in being parsimonious regards his
    person as equal to the world,
You can turn over the world.

[CHAPTER 14]

We look at it but do not see it;
We name this "the minute."
We listen to it but do not hear it;
We name this "the rarefied."
We touch it but do not hold it;
We name this "the level and smooth."

These three cannot be examined to the limit.
Thus they merge together as one.
"One"—there is nothing more encompassing above it,
And nothing smaller below it.
Boundless, formless! It cannot be named,
And returns to the state of no-thing.

This is called the formless form,
The substanceless image.
This is called the subtle and indistinct.
Follow it and you won't see its back;
Greet it and you won't see its head.
Hold on to the Way of the present—
To manage the things of the present,
And to know the ancient beginning.
This is called the beginning of the thread of the Way.

[CHAPTER 15]

The one who was skilled at practicing the Way in
    antiquity,
Was subtle and profound, mysterious and
    penetratingly wise.
His depth cannot be known.
It is only because he cannot be known
That therefore were I forced to describe him I'd say:

Hesitant was he! Like someone crossing a river in
    winter.
Undecided was he! As though in fear of his neighbors
    on all four sides.
Solemn and polite was he! Like a guest.
Scattered and dispersed was he! Like ice as it melts.
Genuine, unformed was he! Like uncarved wood.
Merged, undifferentiated was he! Like muddy water.
Broad and expansive was he! Like a valley.

If you take muddy water and still it, it gradually
    becomes clear.
If you bring something to rest in order to move it, it
    gradually comes alive.
The one who preserves this Way does not desire to be
    full;
Therefore he can wear out with no need to be
    renewed.

[CHAPTER 16]

Take emptiness to the limit;
Maintain tranquility in the center.

The ten thousand things—side-by-side they arise;
And by this I see their return.
Things come forth in great numbers;
Each one returns to its root.
This is called tranquility.
"Tranquility"—This means to return to your fate.
To return to your fate is to be constant;
To know the constant is to be wise.
Not to know the constant is to be reckless and wild;
If you're reckless and wild, your actions will lead to
    misfortune.

To know the constant is to be all-embracing;
To be all-embracing is to be impartial;
To be impartial is to be kingly;
To be kingly is to be like Heaven;
To be like Heaven is to be one with the Tao;
If you're one with the Tao, to the end of your days
    you'll suffer no harm.

[CHAPTER 17]

Chapters 17, 18, and 19 should be read together as a unit.

With the highest kind of rulers, those below simply
    know they exist.
With those one step down—they love and praise them.
With those one further step down—they fear them.
And with those at the bottom—they ridicule and
    insult them.

When trust is insufficient, there will be no trust in
    return.
Hesitant, undecided! Like this is his respect for
    speaking.
He completes his tasks and finishes his affairs,
Yet the common people say, "These things all
    happened by nature."

[CHAPTER 18]

Chapters 17, 18, and 19 should be read together as a unit.

Therefore, when the Great Way is rejected, it is then
   that we have the virtues of humanity and
   righteousness;
When knowledge and wisdom appear, it is then that
   there is great hypocrisy;
When the six relations are not in harmony, it is then
   that we have filial piety and compassion;
And when the country is in chaos and confusion, it is
   then that there are virtuous officials.

[CHAPTER 19]

Chapters 17, 18, and 19 should be read together as a unit.

Eliminate sageliness, throw away knowledge,
And the people will benefit a hundredfold.
Eliminate humanity, throw away righteousness,
And the people will return to filial piety and
   compassion.
Eliminate craftiness, throw away profit,
Then we will have no robbers and thieves.

These three sayings—
Regarded as a text are not yet complete.
Thus, we must see to it that they have the following
   appended:

Manifest plainness and embrace the genuine;
Lessen self-interest and make few your desires;
Eliminate learning and have no undue concern.

[CHAPTER 20]

Agreement and angry rejection;
How great is the difference between them?
Beautiful and ugly;
What's it like—the difference between them?
The one who is feared by others,
Must also because of this fear other men.
Wild, unrestrained! It will never come to an
    end!

The multitudes are peaceful and happy;
Like climbing a terrace in springtime to feast at the
    t'ai-lao sacrifice.
But I'm tranquil and quiet—not yet having given any
    sign.
Like a child who has not yet smiled.
Tired and exhausted—as though I have no place to
    return.
The multitudes all have a surplus.
I alone seem to be lacking.
Mine is the mind of a fool—ignorant and stupid!
The common people see things clearly;
I alone am in the dark.
The common people discriminate and make fine
    distinctions;
I alone am muddled and confused.
Formless am I! Like the ocean;
Shapeless am I! As though I have nothing in which I
    can rest.
The masses all have their reasons for acting;
I alone am stupid and obstinate like a rustic.

But my desires *alone* differ from those of
   others—
For I value drawing sustenance from the Mother.

[CHAPTER 21]

The character of great virtue follows alone from the
   Way.
As for the nature of the Way—it's shapeless and
   formless.
Formless! Shapeless! Inside there are images.
Shapeless! Formless! Inside there are things.
Hidden! Obscure! Inside there are essences.
These essences are very real;
Inside them is the proof.

From the present back to the past,
Its name has never gone away.
It is by this that we comply with the father of the
   multitude of things.
How do I know that the father of the multitude is so?
By this.

[CHAPTER 24]

One who boasts is not established;
One who shows himself off does not become
    prominent;
One who puts himself on display does not brightly
    shine;
One who brags about himself gets no credit;
One who praises himself does not long endure.

In the Way, such things are called:
"Surplus food and redundant action."
And with things—there are those who hate them.
Therefore, the one with the Way in them does not
    dwell.

[CHAPTER 22]

Bent over, you'll be preserved whole;
When twisted, you'll be upright;
When hollowed out, you'll be full;
When worn out, you'll be renewed;
When you have little, you'll attain much;
With much, you'll be confused.

Therefore the Sage holds on to the One and in this
way becomes the shepherd of the world.
He does not show himself off; therefore he becomes
prominent.
He does not put himself on display; therefore he
brightly shines.
He does not brag about himself; therefore he receives
credit.
He does not praise his own deeds; therefore he can
long endure.

It is only because he does not compete that, therefore,
no one is able to compete with him.
The so-called "Bent over you'll be preserved whole" of
the ancients
Was an expression that was really close to it!
Truly "wholeness" will belong to him.

[CHAPTER 23]

To rarely speak—such is the way of Nature.
Fierce winds don't last the whole morning;
Torrential rains don't last the whole day.
Who makes these things?
If even Heaven and Earth can't make these last long—
How much the more is this true for man?!

Therefore, one who devotes himself to the Way is one
    with the Way;
One who devotes himself to Virtue is one with that
    Virtue;
And one who devotes himself to losing is one with that
    loss.
To the one who is one with Virtue, the Way also gives
    Virtue;
While for the one who is one with his loss, the Way
    also disregards him.

[CHAPTER 25]

There was something formed out of chaos,
That was born before Heaven and Earth.
Quiet and still! Pure and deep!
It stands on its own and doesn't change.
It can be regarded as the mother of Heaven and Earth.
I do not yet know its name:
I "style" it "the Way."
Were I forced to give it a name, I would call it "the
   Great."

"Great" means "to depart";
"To depart" means "to be far away";
And "to be far away" means "to return."

The Way is great;
Heaven is great;
Earth is great;
And the king is also great.
In the country there are four greats, and the king
   occupies one place among them.

Man models himself on the Earth;
The Earth models itself on Heaven;
Heaven models itself on the Way;
And the Way models itself on that which is so on its
   own.

[CHAPTER 26]

The heavy is the root of the light;
Tranquility is the lord of agitation.

Therefore the gentleman, in traveling all day, does not
get far away from his luggage carts.
When he's safely inside a walled-in protected hostel
and resting at ease—only then does he transcend
all concern.
How can the king of ten thousand chariots treat his
own person more lightly than the whole land?!

If you regard things too lightly, then you lose the
basic;
If you're agitated, you lose the "lord."

[CHAPTER 27]

The good traveler leaves no track behind;
The good speaker speaks without blemish or flaw;
The good counter doesn't use tallies or chips;
The good closer of doors does so without bolt or lock,
    and yet the door cannot be opened;
The good tier of knots ties without rope or cord, yet
    his knots can't be undone.

Therefore the Sage is constantly good at saving men
    and never rejects anyone;
And with things, he never rejects useful goods.
This is called Doubly Bright.

Therefore the good man is the teacher of the good,
And the bad man is the raw material for the good.
To not value one's teacher and not cherish the raw
    goods—
Though one had great knowledge, he would still be
    greatly confused.
This is called the Essential of the Sublime.

[CHAPTER 28]

When you know the male yet hold on to the female,
You'll be the ravine of the country.
When you're the ravine of the country,
Your constant virtue will not leave.
And when your constant virtue doesn't leave,
You'll return to the state of the infant.

When you know the pure yet hold on to the soiled,
You'll be the valley of the country.
When you're the valley of the country,
Your constant virtue is complete.
And when your constant virtue is complete,
You'll return to the state of uncarved wood.

When you know the white yet hold on to the black,
You'll be the model for the country.
And when you're the model for the country,
Your constant virtue will not go astray.
And when your constant virtue does not go astray,
You'll return to the condition which has no limit.

When uncarved wood is cut up, it's turned into
    vessels;
When the Sage is used, he becomes the Head of
    Officials.
Truly, great carving is done without splitting up.

CHAPTER 29

For those who would like to take control of the world
    and act on it—
I see that with this they simply will not succeed.
The world is a sacred vessel;
It is not something that can be acted upon.
Those who act on it destroy it;
Those who hold on to it lose it.

With things—some go forward, others follow;
Some are hot, others blow cold;
Some are firm and strong, others submissive and weak.
Some rise up while others fall down.
Therefore the Sage:
Rejects the extreme, the excessive, and the
    extravagant.

[CHAPTER 30]

Those who assist their rulers with the Way,
Don't use weapons to commit violence in the world.
Such deeds easily rebound.
In places where armies are stationed, thorns and
  brambles will grow.
The good general achieves his result and that's all;
He does not use the occasion to seize strength from it.

He achieves his result but does not become arrogant;
He achieves his result but does not praise his deeds;
He achieves his result and yet does not brag.
He achieves his result, yet he abides with the result
  because he has no choice.
This is called achieving one's result without using
  force.

When things reach their prime, they get old;
We call this "not the Way."
What is not the Way will come to an early end.

[CHAPTER 31]

As for weapons—they are instruments of ill omen.
And among things there are those that hate them.
Therefore, the one who has the Way, with them does
not dwell.
When the gentleman is at home, he honors the left;
When at war, he honors the right.
Therefore, weapons are not the instrument of the
gentleman—
Weapons are instruments of ill omen.
When you have no choice but to use them, it's best to
remain tranquil and calm.
You should never look upon them as things of beauty.
If you see them as beautiful things—this is to delight
in the killing of men.
And when you delight in the killing of men, you'll not
realize your goal in the land.

Therefore, in happy events we honor the left,
But in mourning we honor the right.
Therefore, the lieutenant general stands on the left;
And the supreme general stands on the right.
Which is to say, they arrange themselves as they would
at a funeral.
When multitudes of people are killed, we stand before
them in sorrow and grief.
When we're victorious in battle, we treat the occasion
like a funeral ceremony.

[CHAPTER 32]

The Tao is constantly nameless.
Though in its natural state it seems small, no one in
    the world dares to treat it as a subject.
Were marquises and kings able to maintain it,
The ten thousand things would submit to them on
    their own,
And Heaven and Earth would unite to send forth
    sweet dew.
By nature it would fall equally on all things, with no
    one among the people ordering that it be so.

As soon as we start to establish a system, we have
    names.
And as soon as there are set names,
Then you must *also* know that it's time to stop.
By knowing to stop—in this way you'll come to no
    harm.
The Way's presence in the world
Is like the relationship of small valley streams to rivers
    and seas.

[CHAPTER 33]

To understand others is to be knowledgeable;
To understand yourself is to be wise.
To conquer others is to have strength;
To conquer yourself is to be strong.
To know when you have enough is to be rich.
To go forward with strength is to have ambition.
To not lose your place is to last long.
To die but not be forgotten—that's true long life.

[CHAPTER 34]

The Way floats and drifts;
It can go left or right.
It accomplishes its tasks and completes its affairs, and
  yet for this it is not given a name.
The ten thousand things entrust their lives to it, and
  yet it does not act as their master.
Thus it is constantly without desires.
It can be named with the things that are small.
The ten thousand things entrust their lives to it, and
  yet it does not act as their master.
It can be named with the things that are great.

Therefore the Sage's ability to accomplish the great
Comes from his not playing the role of the great.
Therefore he is able to accomplish the great.

[CHAPTER 35]

Hold on to the Great Image and the whole world will
    come to you.
Come to you and suffer no harm; but rather know
    great safety and peace.
Music and food—for these passing travelers stop.
Therefore, of the Tao's speaking, we say:
Insipid, it is! It's lack of flavor.
When you look at it, it's not sufficient to be seen;
When you listen to it, it's not sufficient to be heard;
Yet when you use it, it can't be used up.

[CHAPTER 36]

If you wish to shrink it,
You must certainly stretch it.
If you wish to weaken it,
You must certainly strengthen it.
If you wish to desert it,
You must certainly work closely with it.
If you wish to snatch something from it,
You must certainly give something to it.
This is called the Subtle Light.
The submissive and weak conquer the strong.

Fish should not be taken out of the depths;
The state's sharp weapons should not be shown to the
    people.

[CHAPTER 37]

The Tao is constantly nameless.
Were marquises and kings able to maintain it,
The ten thousand things would transform on their
    own.
Having transformed, were their desires to become
    active,
I would subdue them with the nameless simplicity.
Having subdued them with the nameless simplicity,
I would not disgrace them.
By not being disgraced, they will be tranquil.
And Heaven and Earth will of themselves be correct
    and right.

The Way—2,426 characters

PART TWO

TRANSLATION WITH TEXT,
COMMENTARY, AND NOTES

TRANSLATOR'S NOTE

What follows is primarily a translation of Text B of the
Ma-wang-tui texts: the Text A version of a chapter is
used in only seventeen cases—for chapters 1, 31, 42,
43, 44, 45, 46, 50, 51, 52, 56, 61, 62, 63, 69, 76, and
79. In these places what remains of Text A is more
complete, and therefore more readily translated, than
what remains of Text B.

Since Texts A and B are not exactly the same, the
reader might justifiably want to see complete translations of both texts. But the Ma-wang-tui texts do tend
to be alike in places where they differ significantly
from later editions. Thus, translating both would lead
to a lot of repetition. Moreover, Text A is not in good
condition, and any translation of Text A would need to
supply much of the text from some other source to
make the translation readable. Hence my decision has
been to translate that version of each chapter that is
most complete, and in most cases that is the Text B
version. But "Comments and Notes" always begins
with an indication of the ways in which the other text
(normally Text A) differs from the text being translated.

There are lacunae in both texts, the result of material deterioration. In this translation, the missing

words, phrases and lines are supplied in two ways: whenever possible they are from the other Ma-wang-tui text, such words, phrases, and lines being printed in **bold type**. If the other text also has a lacuna at this point, the missing text is supplied from the standard text of *Lao-tzu*, such words, phrases, and lines being printed in *italics*. Any words <u>underlined</u> in the translation are underlined by the present translator for emphasis.

The sequence of chapters in the translation is the sequence we find in the Ma-wang-tui texts. Chapter divisions are made where they occur in modern texts to facilitate reading and comparison. Chapter numbers are put in brackets at the top of the page to remind the reader that these numbers are not found in the original.

For the Chinese text on which this translation is based I have consulted two works, *Ma-wang-tui Han mu po-shu Lao-tzu* (Peking: Wen-wu, 1976), and *Ma-wang-tui Han mu po-shu*, Vol.1 (Peking: Wen-wu, 1980). Whenever there were discrepancies in the transcriptions in these texts I checked the original, using the facsimiles published in the second book.

Please also note that:

1. The transcriptions printed with this translation are those found in *Ma-wang-tui Han-mu po-shu*, Vol.1, as corrected by the present translator. Neither the 1976 nor the 1980 transcription is totally error free. The symbols used in the transcription indicate the following: □—lacuna in the text/character is missing; ○—erroneous character has been blotted out by the copyist; =—what appear to be "ditto" marks in

the original; • —put at the head of a section of text that may be understood by the copyist as a "chapter"; ∠ —indicates a mark in the text that looks like, and seems to serve as, a comma.

2. By the "standard" text of *Lao-tzu*—Chinese commentators often identify this as the *t'ung-hsing pen*—I almost always mean the Wang Pi text of *Lao-tzu* (*Ssu-pu pei-yao* edition).

3. By saying something is "missing" in a Ma-wang-tui text I mean to indicate that there is a lacuna in the text; by contrast, when I note that something is "omitted" or "does not occur" I mean that it was never part of the original.

4. The line numbers used in the translation are not part of the original text: these divisions are made to facilitate discussion in the commentary that follows.

5. In trying to decipher textual variants, I worked carefully through the critical studies of Chou Tz'u-chi (*Lao-tzu k'ao-shu*) and Hsü K'ang-sheng (*Po-shu Lao-tzu chu-shih yü yen-chiu*); I found Hsü K'ang-sheng's work very useful and his arguments often persuasive.

6. Except as noted below, brackets are placed around words which have been supplied by me to make the terse Chinese phraseology more easily understandable.

7. Finally, in my interpretations, and in my choice of words on occasion, I have naturally been influenced by the fine work done on this text by previous translators. To the informed reader my indebtedness to the Wing-tsit Chan and D. C. Lau translations will be obvious.

T E

(VIRTUE)

1 The highest virtue is not virtuous; therefore it truly has virtue.
2 The lowest virtue never loses sight of its virtue; therefore it has no true virtue.

3 The highest virtue takes no action, yet it has no reason for acting this way;
4 The highest humanity takes action, yet it has no reason for acting this way;
5 The highest righteousness takes action, and it has its reasons for acting this way;
6 The highest propriety takes action, and when no one responds to it, then it angrily rolls up its sleeves and forces people to comply.

7 Therefore, when the Way is lost, only then do we have virtue;
8 When virtue is lost, only then do we have humanity;
9 When humanity is lost, only then do we have righteousness;
10 And when righteousness is lost, only then do we have propriety.

11 As for propriety, it's but the thin edge of loyalty and sincerity, and the beginning of disorder.
12 And foreknowledge is but the flower of the Way, and the beginning of stupidity.

13 Therefore the Great Man
14 Dwells in the thick and doesn't dwell in the thin;
15 Dwells in the fruit and doesn't dwell in the flower.
16 Therefore, he rejects that and takes this.

COMMENTS AND NOTES

In line 5, Text B actually begins "The highest virtue" *(shang-te)*, while Text A is like all later editions in having "The highest righteousness" *(shang-i)*. But the character for virtue in Text B has been blotted out, indicating, I think, that the copyist knew he made a mistake. Text A also differs from Text B in seeming to add a line between lines 6 and 7: that line is constructed by having ditto marks follow the words "lost" and "Way," with "Way" being followed by the final particle *i*, and would seem to say "Therefore the Way is lost." This is then followed by "When the Way is lost, only then do we have virtue."

[A]

□□□□□□

德上德无□无以爲也上仁爲之

□以爲也上義爲之而有以爲也上

禮□□□□攘臂而乃之故

失□道□矣而后德失德而后仁失仁

□而義□義而□□道之華也而愚

之首也是以大丈夫居亓厚而不居亓

泊居亓實不居亓華故去皮取此

[B]

上德不德是以有德下德不失德是以

无德上德无爲而无以爲也上仁爲之

而无以爲也上□爲之而有以爲也上

禮爲之而莫之應也則攘臂而乃之故

失道而后德失德而后仁失仁而后義

∠失義而后禮夫禮者忠信之泊也而

乱之首也前識者道之華也而愚之首

也是以大丈夫居□□居亓泊居亓

實而不居亓華故去罷而取此∠

The standard text adds a line between lines 3 and 4, which is "The lowest virtue takes action, and it has its reasons for acting this way." Thus in the standard text the same thing is said of the lowest virtue and the highest righteousness in line 5—they both take action and have their reasons for doing it. It seems clear that a later editor or copyist added this line between 3 and 4 to have the highest virtue balanced by its opposite, lowest virtue, in this sequence, just as it was in lines 1 and 2, but this interrupts the natural flow of lines 3–6, moving from the highest virtue to the highest humanity to the highest righteousness to the highest propriety, and moving from taking no action with no reason for doing so, to taking action but still with no reason, to taking action and having one's reasons, to taking action and then using force. In this way the author shows us what he thinks of the Confucian virtues, ranking them in descending order.

The "foreknowledge" of line 12 is sometimes unclear to readers: It means, I think, in line with the rest of the chapter, to have one's mind made up before one enters a new situation about what is "right" and "wrong" and "proper" and "acceptable" and so on.

[CHAPTER 39]

1 Of those in the past that attained the One—
2 Heaven, by attaining the One became clear;
3 Earth, by attaining the One became stable;
4 Gods, by attaining the One became divine;
5 Valleys, by attaining the One became full;
6 Marquises and kings, by attaining the One made the whole land ordered and secure.[38]

7 Taking this to its logical conclusion we would say—
8 If Heaven were not by means of it clear, it would, I'm afraid, shatter;
9 If the Earth were not by means of it stable, it would, I'm afraid, let go.
10 If the gods were not **by means of it divine, they would**, I'm afraid, be powerless.
11 If valleys were not by means of it **full**, they would, [**I'm afraid,**] dry up.
12 And if marquises and kings were not by means of it noble and high, they would, I'm afraid, topple and fall.

13 Therefore, it must be the case that the noble has the base as its root;
14 And it must be the case that the high has the low for its foundation.
15 Thus, for this reason, marquises and kings call themselves "The Orphan," "The Widower," and "The One Without Grain."[39]
16 This is taking the base as one's root, is it not?!

17 Therefore, they regard their large numbers of carriages as having no carriage.
18 And because of this, they desire not to dazzle and glitter like jade,
19 But to remain firm and strong like stone.

COMMENTS AND NOTES

Text A omits "the whole land" *(t'ien-hsia)* in line 6, and in Text A, the word *wei*—"we would say" or "it would mean that"—which occurs at the end of line 7 (or the start of line 8), is repeated at the start of lines 9–12.

The particle *erh* ("and yet") in the middle of lines 13 and 14 in

昔之得一者天得一以清地得□以寧
神得一以靈浴得一以盈侯□□而
以為正亓致之也胃天毋已清將恐□
胃地毋□將恐□胃神毋已霝將恐
歇胃浴毋已盈將恐渴胃侯王毋已
貴□□故必貴而以賤為本必
高矣而以下為亓夫是以侯王自胃
孤寡不榖此亓賤□□與非□故致數
與无與是故不欲□□若玉硌＝
□□

昔得一者天得一以清地得一以寧神
得一以霝浴得一以盈侯王得一以為天
下正亓至也胃天毋已清將恐蓮地毋
□寧將恐發神毋□□恐歇谷毋已
□將渴侯王毋已貴以高將恐坎故必
貴以賤為本必高矣而以下為亓夫是
以侯王自胃孤寡不榖此亓賤之本與
非也故至數與无與是故不欲祿＝若
玉硌＝ 若石

Text A (but only in line 14 in B) suggests a possible reading of "Therefore, it must be the case that *even though* they are noble, *nonetheless*, they take the base as their root; And it must be the case that *even though* they are high, *nonetheless*, they have the low for their foundation."

Most versions of the *Lao-tzu* add a line between 5 and 6 ("The myriad things obtained the One and lived and grew"), and a parallel line between 11 and 12 ("If the myriad things had not thus lived and grown, They would soon become extinct"[40]). Also, the *chih-chih* ("arrive at it" or "extreme it") in line 7, followed by "the One" *(i yeh)*

[105]

instead of "we would say" *(wei)*, has led us to read this line as "The thing that helped them to arrive at this state was the One" rather than "Taking this to its logical conclusion we would say."

In lines 8–12 the Ma-wang-tui texts use the final *i* ("and that's all" or "completely/finally"), where the standard text has the instrumental *i* ("by this means," "using this") nevertheless, the meaning remains unchanged.[41]

The word "must" *(pi)* is added to lines 13 and 14 in the Ma-wang-tui texts, and line 16 is grammatically slightly different, the standard text using two negatives to make the same point—"Is this not regarding humble station as the basis of honor? Is it not? "[42]

Finally, the meaning of the last three lines remains problematic, though the argument that the word "carriage" *(yü)* in line 17 is a corruption of an original *yü* meaning "praise" seems less likely since it is "carriage" we find in Text B.[43] Following the reading of "carriage," Chan translates: "Therefore enumerate all the parts of a chariot as you may, and you still have no chariot." This would presumably mean that a distinction is being drawn between the whole and the sum of its parts. D. C. Lau, reading *"yü"* as "praise," has "Thus the highest renown is without renown."[44] Neither interpretation seems to follow from what went before, and in my translation, therefore, I have followed the lead of Cheng Liang-shu.[45]

[CHAPTER 41]

1 When the highest type of *men hear* the Way, with diligence
they're able to practice it;

2 When average men hear the Way, some things they retain and
others they lose;

3 When the lowest type of men hear the Way, they laugh out loud
at it.

4 If they didn't laugh at it, *it couldn't* be regarded as the Way.

5 Therefore, there is a set saying about this that goes:

6 The bright Way appears to be dark;

7 The Way that goes forward appears to retreat;

8 The smooth Way appears to be uneven;

9 The highest virtue [is empty] like a valley;

10 The purest white appears to be soiled;

11 Vast virtue appears to be insufficient;

12 Firm virtue appears *thin and weak*;

13 The simplest *reality appears to change.*

14 The Great Square has no corners;

15 The Great Vessel takes long to complete;

16 The Great Tone makes little sound;

17 The Great Image has no shape.

18 The Way is Great but has no name.

19 Only the Way is good at beginning things and also good at
bringing things to completion.

COMMENTS AND NOTES

All that remains of Text A are the words "the Way is good at" *(tao-shan)* in line 19.

Line 1 is slightly different from the standard text: the Ma-wang-tui text has "with diligence *they are able* to practice it" *(ch'in neng hsing-chih)* where the standard text says "they work diligently at it *and* practice it" *(ch'in erh hsing-chih).* Also, in line 6, where the standard text has *mei* for "dark," Text B has *fei* ("extravagant" or "wasteful"), but I follow Hsü K'ang-sheng in reading this as the *fei* which means "poor eyesight,"[46] and in this way arrive at "things being in the dark."

In line 18 the Ma-wang-tui text says the Way is "Great" *(pao)* instead of "hidden" *(yin).* And in line 19 the Ma-wang-tui text has

[A]

[B]

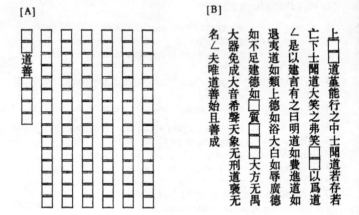

上□□道堇能行之中　士聞道若存若
亡下士聞道大笑之弗笑□□以爲道
∠是以建言有之曰明道如費進道如
退夷道如類上德如浴大白如辱廣德
如不足建德如□質□□大方无禺
大器免成大音希聲天象无刑道襃无
名∠夫唯道善始且善成

道善□

"begin" (shih) in place of "bestow" or "give" (tai) and adds a shan ("is good at") before the word "complete" at the end of the line. D. C. Lau's translation of the standard text reads, "It is the way alone that excels in bestowing and in accomplishing."[47]

[108]

[CHAPTER 40]

1 "Reversal" is the movement of the Tao;
2 **"Weakness"** is the function of the Tao.

3 The things of the world originate in being,
4 And being *originates* in nonbeing.

COMMENTS AND NOTES

In line 3, the Ma-wang-tui texts have simply "the things" *(wu)* where
the standard text has "the ten thousand things" *(wan-wu).*

[B]

反也者道之動也□之□者道之用也天
下之物生於有、□於无

[A]

□□□□□□□□□

□道之動也弱也者道之用也天

1 **The Way gave birth to the One.**
2 **The One gave birth to the Two.**
3 **The Two gave birth to the Three.**
4 **And the Three gave birth to** *the ten thousand things.*
5 *The ten thousand things carry Yin on their backs and wrap their arms around Yang.*
6 Through the blending of ch'i they arrive at a state of harmony.

7 The things that are hated by the whole world
8 Are to be orphaned, widowed, and have no grain.
9 Yet kings and dukes take these as their names.
10 Thus with all things—some *are increased* by taking away;
11 While some are diminished by *adding on.*

12 Therefore, *what* other men teach,
13 [I] will also consider and then teach to others.
14 Thus, "The strong and violent do not come to a natural end."
15 **I will** take this as the father of my studies.

COMMENTS AND NOTES

(For the meaning of lines 8–9, see note 39.) Missing from Text B are lines 5, 10, 12–14, and portions of lines 4, 6, and 15. In what survives, it is clear that lines 10–11 were reversed in Text B. That is to say, they said, "Thus with all things—some are diminished by adding on, while some are increased by taking away." Also, in line 7, Text B agrees with the standard text in having "what *people* hate" *(jen)* not "the whole world" *(t'ien-hsia).*

The "therefores" at the beginning of lines 12 and 14 are not found in the standard text. And the Ma-wang-tui texts have "studies" *(hsüeh)* in the last line where most editions have "teachings" *(chiao).*

Line 13 assumes a form in the Ma-wang-tui texts that we do not find in other editions. Normally the line simply reads, "I will also teach it" *(wo i chiao-chih).* The Ma-wang-tui text has *hsi i erh chiao-jen* (literally—"evening consider and then teach others"). I read the *hsi* ("evening") as *i* ("also"), since the archaic pronunciations of the two were close *(dziak* and *ziak* respectively). Quite a few editions of the *Lao-tzu* have a line that is close to what we find in the Ma-wang-tui text—*i wo i chiao-chih* ("is also my meaning when teaching them").[48]

[B]

道生一一生二二生三三生□□□□□□

□□□□□□以爲和人之所亞唯

孤寡不䅵而王公以自□□□□□□

□云二之而益□□□□□□

□□□□□□吾將以□□父

[A]

□□□□□□中氣以爲和天下之所惡

唯孤寡不䅵而王公以自名也勿或敗

之□□之而敗故人□□教夕議而

教人故强良者不得死我□以爲學父

[112]

[CHAPTER 43, *TEXT A*]

1 The softest, most pliable thing in the world **runs** roughshod over the firmest thing in the world.
2 That which has no substance gets into that which has no spaces or cracks.
3 I therefore know *that there is* benefit in taking no action.
4 The *wordless* teaching, the benefit of taking no action—
5 Few in the world can realize these!

COMMENTS AND NOTES

It becomes clear in chapter 78—if it is not clear here—that the softest thing in the world is water and the firmest is rock.

Not much remains of Text B beyond line 1. The Ma-wang-tui version of this chapter is exactly the same as what we find in other texts, with the exception of the inclusion of a few grammatical particles, which make the syntax more precise.

天下之至柔□專於天下之致堅无有
人於无間五是以知无爲□□益也不
□□教无爲之益□下希能及之矣

矣

天下之至□馳騁乎天下□□
□□□无間吾是以□
也不□□□□□□□□□□□

1 Fame or your health—which is more dear?
2 Your health or possessions—which is worth more?
3 Gain or loss—in which is there harm?
4 *If your desires are great, you're bound to be extravagant;*
5 *If you store much away, you're bound* to lose *a great deal.*
6 Therefore, if you know contentment, you'll not be disgraced.
7 If you know when to stop, you'll suffer no harm.
8 And in this way you can last a very long time.

COMMENTS AND NOTES

Text B has been completely lost save for the opening words of line 1 ("fame or"). The standard *Lao-tzu* text has a "therefore" at the start of line 4 but does not have one at the start of line 6. In all other ways the Ma-wang-tui text is the same as the standard text.

[A]

名與身孰親身與貨孰多得與亡孰病
甚□□□亡故知足不辱
知止不殆可以長久

[B]

名與□□□□□□□□□□
□□□□□□□□□
□□□□□□□

[CHAPTER 45, *TEXT A*]

1 Great completion seems incomplete;
2 Yet its usefulness is never exhausted.
3 Great fullness seems to be empty;
4 Yet its usefulness is never used up.
5 Great straightness seems to be bent.
6 Great skill seems to be clumsy.
7 Great surplus seems to stammer.
8 Activity overcomes cold;
9 Tranquility overcomes heat.
10 If you're quiet and tranquil you can become the ruler of the
   world.

COMMENTS AND NOTES

Text B has "lacking" *(ch'u)* at the end of line 7 instead of "stammer" (reading *nen* ["heat"] in Text A as *na)*, and the lacuna in Text B at this point seems to allow for another line between lines 6 and 7. Since the standard text has "Great eloquence seems to stammer" for line 7, it would appear that Text B originally read, "Great eloquence seems to stammer; Great surplus seems to be lacking." These two lines were apparently reversed in the text copied by copyist A, and he proceeded to collapse the two, resulting in the nonsensical line "Great surplus seems to stammer." Hsü K'ang-sheng makes the case for two lines here in Text B,[49] and D. C. Lau also restores these two lines.[50]

[A]

大成若缺亓用不幣大盈若盅亓用不
䆮大直如詘大巧如拙大贏如炳䟴勝
寒䚮勝灵請䚮可以爲天下正

[B]

□
□

□絀遾朕寒□□□□□□

□巧如掘□□□□

□盈如沖元□□□□□□□

[CHAPTER 46, *TEXT A*]

1 When the world has the Way, ambling horses **are retired** to fertilize [fields].
2 When the world lacks the Way, war horses are reared in the suburbs.

3 Of crimes—none is greater than having things that one desires;
4 Of disasters—none is greater than not knowing when one has enough.
5 Of defects—none brings more sorrow than the desire to attain.
6 *Therefore, the contentment one has when he knows that he has enough*, is abiding contentment indeed.

COMMENTS AND NOTES

"Periods" (chapter markers?) occur at the start of lines 1 and 3 in Text A. The word "world" *(t'ien-hsia)* is omitted from line 2 in Text B, giving "When *it* lacks the Way . . ."

Line 3 does not occur in the Wang Pi text of the *Lao-tzu*, but it is commonly found in other editions. There is a common gloss of the *k'o-yü* ("the desirable") in the line that reads it as *to-yü* ("many desires").[51] With this change the line would read, "Of crimes—none is greater than having many desires."

In line 5, most texts parallel lines 3 and 4 by saying "Of defects—*none is greater than* the desire to attain" *(mo ta yü)*, versus the Ma-wang-tui phrase "nothing brings more sorrow than . . ." *(mo ts'an yü)*.

□□道却走馬□糞无道戎馬生於

郊罪莫大可欲禍□□□□□

□□□□□□□□□□足矣

· 天下有道□走馬以糞天下无道戎

馬生於郊 · 罪莫大於可欲醧莫大於

不知足咎莫憯於欲得□□□□□□恒

足矣

[CHAPTER 47]

1 No need to leave your door to know the whole world;
2 No need to peer through **your windows to** know the Way of Heaven.
3 The farther you go, the *less* you know.

4 *Therefore the Sage knows without going,*
5 Names *without seeing,*
6 And completes without doing a thing.

COMMENTS AND NOTES

The Ma-wang-tui texts are the same as the standard text for this chapter, though they are grammatically more complete and therefore more precise.

The negative in the last line—*fu*—posits an object to the verb it precedes—hence my "without doing *a thing*." It is conceivable that the negatives in lines 4 and 5 were *fu* as well in the Ma-wang-tui texts. That would give us a reading of: "Therefore the Sage knows things without going *to them*; names things without seeing *them*, and completes things without doing *a thing*."

[122]

[B]

不出於户以知天下不規於□□知天

道元出寶遠者元知簡□□□

□□□□而名弗爲而成

[A]

不出於户以知天下不規於牖以知天

道元出也殹遠元□□□□□

□□□□□□□弗爲而□

[CHAPTER 48]

1 Those who work at their studies increase day after day;
2 Those who have heard the Tao decrease day after day.
3 They decrease and decrease, till they get to the point where they
  do nothing.
4 *They do nothing and yet there's nothing left undone.*
5 *When someone wants to* take control of the world, he must always
  be unconcerned with affairs.
6 For in a case where he's concerned with affairs,
7 *He'll be un*worthy, *as well*, of taking control of the *world*.

COMMENTS AND NOTES

Only six characters remain from Text A in this chapter.

The particle *che* ("the one who/those who") in lines 1 and 2 in
the Ma-wang-tui text better supports the present translation than one
in which the lines are treated like definitions (e.g., Wing-tsit Chan
translates the standard text: "The pursuit of learning is to increase
day after day. The pursuit of Tao is to decrease day after day."[52]) The
Ma-wang-tui variant "hear/heard" *(wen)* in line 2 instead of "do" or
"pursue" *(wei)* is unattested elsewhere.

On line 4, see the notes to chapter 37 below.

The "when someone wants to" *(chiang-yü)* at the start of
line 5 is the reading in the Fu I and Yen Tsun texts.[53] The word
"therefore" *(ku)* is also common in this place. Also, the instrumental
i at the end of line 5 in the standard text (that is, "he must always
use being unconcerned with affairs") does not occur here.

[A] [B]

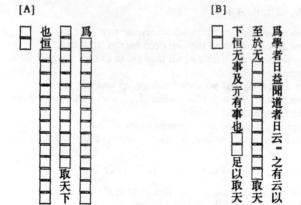

[124]

[CHAPTER 49]

1 *The Sage* constantly has no [set] mind;
2 He takes the mind of the common people as his mind.
3 **Those who** are good **he regards as good;**
4 **Those who are not good he also regards as good.**
5 [In this way] *he attains* goodness.
6 Those who are trustworthy he trusts;
7 And those who are not trustworthy he also trusts.
8 [In this way] he gets their trust.
9 As for the Sage's presence in the world—he is one with it.
10 **And with the world he merges his mind.**
11 **The common** people all fix their **eyes and ears on him.**
12 **And the Sage treats them all as his children.**

COMMENTS AND NOTES

Texts A and B are in equally poor condition: lines 1, 5, 6, and 7 are all missing from Text A.

The words "constant" and "without" in line 1 are reversed in the standard text, giving "The Sage is without a constant mind [of his own]."

The first-person pronoun "I" *(wu)* is found in the standard text in lines 3, 4, 6, and 7, making the author "the Sage." Thus they read, "Those who are good *I* regard as good; Those who are not good *I* also regard as good," and so on.

The addition of the grammatical particle *yen* ("with it," "on him") at the end of lines 9 and 11 greatly clarifies the meaning.

Line 11 does not occur in all texts.

[B]

□人恒无心以百省之心爲心善□

□□□善也信者信之不

信者亦信之德信也耶人之在天下也

欱□□焉□□□生皆注元□

□□□□□

[A]

□□□□□□

□□以百□之心爲□善者善

之不善者亦善□□□□□□□

□□□□信也□□□之在天下翕

□焉爲天下渾心百姓皆屬耳目爲聖

人皆咳之

1 *We come out into* life **and go back into death.**
2 *The companions* of **life** *are thirteen;*
3 The companions of *death* are thirteen;
4 And yet people, because they regard life as LIFE, in all of their actions move toward the thirteen that belong to the realm of death.
5 Now, why is this so?
6 It's because they regard life as LIFE.

7 You've no doubt **heard of** those who are **good at** holding on to life:
8 When walking through hills, they don't **avoid** rhinos and tigers;
9 When they go into battle, they don't put on armor or shields;
10 The rhino has no place to probe with its horn;
11 The tiger finds no place to put its claws.
12 And weapons find no place to hold *their blades.*
13 *Now,* why is this so?
14 Because there is no place for death in them.

COMMENTS AND NOTES

The Ma-wang-tui texts contain a number of interesting variants. In line 7, the standard text has those who are good at "taking care of" *(she)* their lives, where the Ma-wang-tui texts have "holding on to" *(chih)* their lives. In line 8, the standard text has "on dry land" *(lu)* instead of through the "hills" *(ling)*. Also in line 8, the standard text says they won't "meet up with" *(yü)* rhinos and tigers instead of "avoid" *(pi)*. In line 10, where the Ma-wang-tui texts have "probe" *(ch'uai)*, the standard text has "throw" *(t'ou)*. The *yen* ("in them") at the end of line 14 does not normally occur, though it is a known variant. Finally, line 6 in the standard text reads, "It's because they too intently regard life as LIFE"; the "too intently" comes from adding the characters *chih-hou* to the end of the Ma-wang-tui line (i.e., *i ch'i sheng-sheng chih-hou).*

The "thirteen" in lines 2–4 are variously identified as the four limbs and nine cavities in the body, or the four passages (ears, eyes, nose, and mouth) and the nine cavities, or the seven emotions (delight, anger, grief, fear, love, hate, and desire) and the six desires (of the eye, ear, nose, tongue, body, and mind).[54]

By no means is there universal agreement that the *shih-yu san* in

[A]

何故也以亓无死地焉

亓角虎无所昔亓蚤兵无所容□□

行不□矢虎入軍不被甲兵矢无所椯

何故也以亓生= 也蓋□□執生者陵

三而民生= 勤皆之死地之十有三夫

□生□□□有□□徒十有

[B]

□也以亓无

□□□□□□□□□亓蚤兵

行不辟累虎入軍不被兵革累无□□

□何故也以亓生= 蓋聞善執生者陵

三而民生= 生僮皆之死地之十有三

□生入死生之□□□之徒十又

---

lines 2–4 should be read as "thirteen"; in fact the preferred reading is, rather, "three out of ten." Thus Wing-tsit Chan translates these lines, "Three out of ten are companions of life. Three out of ten are companions of death. And three out of ten in their lives lead from activity to death."[55] I like this interpretation and take it to mean that, roughly speaking, one-third of humanity seems to be born to live and will live a long time no matter what they do; another third seems born fated to die and will die young no matter what they do; and finally, another third can live long or die young depending on how they live, but they hasten their journey to death with their anxiety to hold on to life.

It is with some reluctance, therefore, that I adopt the "thirteen" reading, and I do so based in part on internal evidence from elsewhere in the text, and in part on the grammatical form of these lines in the Ma-wang-tui texts.

The internal evidence is that in chapter 76 there is mention once again of the "companions" of life and death *(sheng chih t'u, ssu chih t'u)*, and there "companions" means the *qualities of the body* in life or death (suppleness and softness, or rigidity and firmness), not different groups of people. The grammatical evidence from the Ma-wang-tui texts is (a) that line 4 begins "And yet people" *(erh min*—the *erh* does not occur in the standard text), seeming to indicate that two alternatives have been presented, the good one being obvious, *and yet* people end up choosing the other, and (b) where the standard text has *i* ("also") at the end of line 4 (i.e., it says, "These are also 'thirteen' [or 'three out of ten']," supporting the idea that there are three different groups being discussed), the Ma-wang-tui texts have the possessive particle *chih*, giving the reading of "the thirteen (or three out of ten) that belong to the realm of death" (literally "death realm's thirteen").[56]

I might add, to further this claim, that *shih-yu X* as "ten has [=plus] X" is a form we find in other early texts.[57] In Confucius' well-known words in *Analects* 2:4—"At the age of fifteen, I set my heart on learning"—"fifteen" is *shih-yu wu*.

[CHAPTER 51, *TEXT A*]

1 The Way gives birth to them and Virtue nourishes them;

2 Substance gives them form and their unique capacities complete them.

3 Therefore the ten thousand things venerate the Way and honor **Virtue**.

4 As for their veneration of **the Way** and their honoring of Virtue—

5 No one rewards them for it; it's constantly so on its own.

6 The Way gives birth to them, nourishes them, matures them, completes them, rests them, **rears** them, **supports them, and protects** *them*.

7 *It gives birth to them but* doesn't try to own them;

8 It acts on their behalf but doesn't make them dependent;

9 It matures them but doesn't rule them.

10 This we call Profound Virtue.

COMMENTS AND NOTES

"Periods" occur at the start of lines 1 and 6 in Text A. Texts A and B differ in minor grammatical ways; these differences do not affect the meaning or the translation.

The Ma-wang-tui texts contain a number of interesting variants. To begin with, in line 2 they have "unique capacities" or "talents" *(ch'i)* where the standard text has "circumstances" or "conditions" *(shih)*. Then in line 3 they omit the words "none does not" *(mo pu)*, which make the standard text read, "Of the ten thousand things, none does not venerate . . ."

In line 5 the Ma-wang-tui texts have "reward" (literally "give noble rank to"—*chüeh*) where the standard text has "order" *(ming)*, but *chüeh* is a known and common variant.

A "therefore" at the head of line 6 in the standard text is omitted here. Also in line 6, in the standard text it is again "Virtue" that "nourishes them, matures them . . . ," and so on. The word "Virtue" is omitted in the Ma-wang-tui texts, as it is in many other editions of the text as well.

謂玄德

弗有也爲而弗寺也長而勿宰也此之
之長之遂之亭之□之□□□□□
也夫莫之尌而恒自然也 · 道生之畜
是以萬物尊道而貴□□之尊德之貴
 · 道生之而德畜之物刑之而器成之

道生之德畜之物刑之而器成之是以
萬物尊道而貴德道之尊也德之貴也
夫莫之爵也而恒自然也道生之畜□
□□之亭之毒之養之復□□□□
□□□□□□□弗宰是胃玄德

[CHAPTER 52, *TEXT A*]

1 The world had a beginning,
2 Which can be considered the mother of the world.
3 Having attained the mother, in order to understand her
   children,
4 If you return and hold on to the mother, till the end of your life
   you'll suffer no harm.

5 Block up the holes;[58]
6 Close the doors;
7 And till the end of your life you'll not labor.
8 Open the holes;
9 Meddle in affairs;
10 And till the end of your life **you'll not be saved.**[59]

11 **To perceive** the small is called **"discernment."**
12 To hold on to the pliant is called "strength."
13 If you use the rays to return to the bright light,
14 You'll not abandon your life to peril.
15 This is called Following the Constant.

COMMENTS AND NOTES

Lines 13 and 14 seem to parallel line 4 and the second half of line 3 above: thus one avoids harm by "knowing the children" but "returning to the mother," and in like fashion one avoids peril by using the rays *(kuang)* to trace one's way back to the source of the light *(ming*—i.e., the Tao). But remember that there is a "period" at the head of line 5 in Text A, possibly indicating that the copyist or an editor saw no connection between lines 1–4 and what follows.

Text B is like the standard text in adding a phrase between lines 3 and 4: "And having known the children." Actually it says, "And having *returned* to know the children," but the "returned" *(fu)* is smudged, indicating that the copyist realized he had made a mistake.

[A]

明毋道身央是胃襲常

□小曰□守柔曰强用亓光復歸亓

亓門終身不堇啓亓悶濟亓事終身□

亓□復守亓母沒身不殆・塞亓闘閉

天下有始以爲天下母既得亓母以知

[B]

□□□□□遺身央是胃□常

□□不棘見小曰明守□□強用□

塞亓兌閉亓門冬身不堇啓亓兌齊亓

亓子既○知亓子復守亓母沒身不佁

天下有始以爲天下母既得亓母以知

[CHAPTER 53]

1 Were I to have the least bit of knowledge,[60] in walking on a Great Road, it's only going astray that I would fear.
2 The Great Way is very level;
3 But people greatly delight in tortuous paths.

4 The courts are swept very clean;
5 While the fields are full of weeds;
6 And the granaries are all empty.
7 Their clothing—richly embroidered and colored;
8 While at their waists they carry sharp swords.
9 They gorge themselves on food, and of possessions and goods *they have plenty.*

10 *This is called* thievery!
11 *And thievery* certainly isn't *the Way!*

COMMENTS AND NOTES

Roughly one-third of Text A is now missing (lines 10 and 11 and parts of 1 and 2). But the "period" at the head of line 1 is clear.

At the end of line 3 the Ma-wang-tui texts do not have the standard *ching* ("narrow path" or "byway") but rather a character that seems best identified as the word meaning "small path through a mountain valley."[61]

In line 9 the standard text says they (i.e., rich nobles/ruling aristocracy) gorge themselves on food *and drink* (versus just food in the Ma-wang-tui texts).

In line 11, the Ma-wang-tui texts seem to have been like the Fu I text in repeating the "thievery" *(tao hsi)* from line 10; those two characters are normally left out.

The author makes a pun in the last two lines: "thievery" and "the Way" are both pronounced *tao* (fourth tone); that is, the lines read, "This is called tao! And this tao certainly isn't *the* tao!"

One of the principles followed by the editor or editors who arranged the text in its present sequence was to have sections of text that use the same word or words follow one another. Here the first three lines may or may not connect well with what follows, but in both blocks of material the word "very" *(shen)* is a point of focus. Lines 2 and 3 literally say "great way *very* level, people *very much* like tortuous paths" while lines 4–6 literally read "courts *very* clean, fields *very* weedy, granaries *very* empty."

・使我摞有知也□□大道唯□□

□其夷／民甚好解／朝甚除／田

甚芜／倉甚虛服文采帶利□□食／

貨□□□□□□□□□□□□□□□

使我介有知行於大道唯他是畏大道

甚夷民甚好儌朝甚除田甚芜倉甚虛

服文采帶利劍厭食而齎財□□□

盜□□□非□也

[135]

[CHAPTER 54]

1   What is firmly set up *can't be* **pulled down**;
2   *What is firmly embraced cannot slip free.*
3   And your sons and grandsons, as a result, will sacrifice without end.

4   When you cultivate it in your person, your virtue will then be genuine;
5   When you cultivate it in your family, your virtue will then overflow;
6   When you cultivate it in your village, your virtue will then be long lasting;
7   When you cultivate it in your state, your virtue will then be abundant;
8   And when you cultivate it throughout the world, your virtue will then be widespread.

9   Use the individual to examine the individual;
10   Use the family to examine **the family**;
[10a **Use the village to examine the village**;]
11   **Use the state to examine** the state;
12   And use the world to examine the world;
13   How do I know that the world is so?
14   By *this*.

COMMENTS AND NOTES

Text A, like the standard text, has an additional line between lines 10 and 11—"Use the village to examine the village." This is incorrectly omitted in Text B. All that remains from Text A are lines 9–11 (with the added line) and parts of lines 3 and 12.

The Ma-wang-tui version of this chapter is essentially the same as we find in other texts with the exception of a few synonym substitutions here and there: for example, at the end of line 3 the Ma-wang-tui texts have *chüeh* ("to end," "be cut off ") instead of the normal *cho* ("stop," "cease"), and at the end of line 8 they say virtue will be "widespread" (*po*) instead of "universal" (*p'u*).

[A]

善建□□撥□□□□□□□子孫以祭祀

餘脩之□□□□□以身□身以家觀家

以鄉觀鄉以邦觀邦以天□觀□□□

[B]

善建者□□□□□□□□子孫以祭祀

不絶脩之身亓德乃真脩之家亓德有

餘脩之鄉亓德乃長脩之國亓德乃

脩之天下亓德乃博以身觀身以家觀

□□□國以天下觀天下吾何□知

天下之然茲以□

[137]

[CHAPTER 55]

1 One who embraces the fullness of Virtue,
2 Can be compared to a newborn babe.
3 Wasps and scorpions, snakes and vipers do not sting him;
4 Birds of prey and fierce beasts do not seize him;
5 His bones and muscles are weak and pliant, yet his grasp is firm;
6 He does not yet know the meeting of male and female, yet his
   organ is aroused—
7 This is because his essence is at its height.
8 He can scream all day, yet he won't become hoarse—
9 **This is because his** harmony **is at its height**.

10 *To know* **harmony is called** "the constant";
11 To know the constant is called "being wise";
12 To add on to life **is called** a "bad omen";
13 For the mind to control the breath—that's called "forcing
   things."

14 When things *reach their prime* they get old;
15 This is called "not the Way."
16 What is not the Way will come to an early end.

COMMENTS AND NOTES

In line 5, Text A is like the standard text in having "His bones are weak and his muscles are pliant." In line 10, Text A has simply "Harmony is called 'the constant.'"

For line 4 the Ma-wang-tui texts have a six-character sentence that parallels line 3; the standard text makes two clauses out of this and reverses the "birds of prey" and the "fierce beasts"; thus, Wing-tsit Chan translates, "Fierce beasts will not seize him. Birds of prey will not strike him."[62]

In line 6 the Ma-wang-tui texts have the "meeting" *(hui)* of male and female where other texts have the synonymous "union" *(ho)*. And in agreement with most editions of the text, in line 6 in the Ma-wang-tui texts it is the child's "organ" ("penis"—*tsui*) that is aroused, not his "perfection" *(ch'üan*—as in the Wang Pi text).

Line 14 might seem to be at odds with the "natural" way of the Taoists. But I think the point is that when people reach their prime, they are inclined to want more of life, to show off their strength, and to use their minds to control their lives (lines 12 and 13). But this

[B]

含德之厚者比於赤子蠭蠆虫蛇弗赫
據鳥孟獸弗捕骨筋弱柔而握固∠
未知牝牡之會而朘怒精之至也冬日
號而□□□□□□常知日
明益生□祥心使氣曰强物□則老胃
之不∟道∟蚤已

[A]

□之厚□比於赤子逢㵟蠆地弗螫
攫鳥猛獸弗搏骨弱筋柔而握固未知
牝牡□□而朘□精□至也∠終日號
而不嗄和之至也和曰常知和曰明
益生曰祥∠心使氣曰强□□即老胃
之不∟道∟□□□

leads to using up and wasting away one's vital powers and hence the
start of old age. (On these lines see also chapter 30, below.)

[139]

[CHAPTER 56, TEXT A]

1 **Those who know** don't talk about it; those who talk don't know it.

2 He blocks up his holes,
3 Closes his **doors**,
4 **Softens** the glare,
5 Settles the dust,
6 Files down the sharp edges,
7 And unties the tangles.
8 This is called Profound Union.

9 Therefore, there is no way to get intimate with him,
10 But there is also no way to shun him.
11 There is no way to benefit him,
12 But there is also no way to harm him.
13 There is no **way** to ennoble him,
14 But there is also no way to debase him.
15 For this very reason he's the noblest thing in the world.

COMMENTS AND NOTES

The "And" *(erh)* at the head of line 7 is explicit in Text B (but not in Text A). In line 11, the copyist for Text B skipped ahead one line by mistake before correcting the error: as a result, Text B literally says, "There is no way to *harm and* benefit him."

In line 1 the difference between the standard text—which says, "Those who know don't speak, and those who speak don't know"—is a difference in the negative used: the standard text uses *pu* ("not," "don't") whereas the Ma-wang-tui texts have *fu* ("not ——— it" "don't ——— it").

Lines 2–7 in the Ma-wang-tui texts follow a different sequence than we normally find. In the standard text the order is 2, 3, 6, 7, 4, 5. Lines 2 and 3 occur above in chapter 52, and lines 4–7 (in the order 6, 7, 4, 5) are also found in chapter 4.

The "also"s in lines 10, 12, and 14 do not occur in the standard *Lao-tzu* text, but they are attested in a small number of other editions.

[B]

知者弗言 = 者弗知塞亓兑閉亓門和
亓光同亓塵銼亓兑而解亓紛是胃玄
同故不可得而親也亦□□得而
□得而○利□□□得而害不可得而
貴亦不可得而賤故爲天下貴

[A]

□弗言 = 者弗知∠塞亓悶閉亓□
□其光同亓塵坐亓閱解亓紛是胃玄
同∠故不可得而親亦不可得而疏∠
不可得而利亦不可得而害不可□而
貴亦不可得而淺故爲天下貴

CHAPTER 57

1 Use the upright and correct to order the state;
2 Use surprise tactics when you use troops;
3 Use unconcern with affairs to take control of the world.

4 How do I know that this is so?
5 Well, the more taboos and prohibitions there are in the world,
   the poorer the people will be;
6 The more sharp weapons the people possess, **the more
   muddled the states will be;**
7 **The more knowledge** *and skill* **people have, the more novel
   things** *will appear;*
8 The more *legal* matters are made prominent, *the more* robbers
   and thieves *there will be.*

9 Therefore, the words of the *Sage* say:
10 I do nothing, and the people of themselves are transformed;
11 I love tranquility, and the people of themselves are upright;
12 I'm unconcerned with affairs, and the people of themselves
   become rich;
13 I desire not to desire, and the people of themselves are [genuine
   and simple, like] uncarved wood.

COMMENTS AND NOTES

For the reconstruction of line 7 in Text B I have followed Cheng
Liang-shu.[63] Text A omits the word "skill" *(ch'iao)*; the standard text
has "talent and skill" *(chi-ch'iao)*, but the reading of "knowledge and
skill" *(chih-ch'iao)* is also attested.[64] There is a "period" at the start
of line 1 in Text A.

In the standard text, the question raised in line 4 is answered:
"By this" *(i-tz'u)*. Also, the *fu* ("Well,") at the start of line 5 does not
occur.

In line 8 the standard text has "laws and commands" *(fa-ling)* in
place of "legal matters" *(fa-wu*—an attested reading), and in line 9,
the standard reading is "Therefore the Sage says" *(ku sheng-jen yün)*.

Finally, all other editions of the *Lao-tzu* have "I have no desires" *(wo wu-yü)* in the last line where the Ma-wang-tui texts say, "I
desire not to desire" *(wo yü pu-yü)*.

Waley, correctly I feel, notes that line 2 is surely a maxim of the
Strategists (or Militarists—*ping-chia*) that the present author is

[A]

　·以正之邦以畸用兵以无事取天下
吾何□□也戋夫天下□諱而
民彌貧／民多利器而邦家茲昏人多
知而何物茲□□□盗賊□
我无爲也而民自化
我好静而民自正我无事民□□□□□

[B]

以正之國以畸用兵以無事取天下吾
何以知亓然也才夫天下多忌諱而民
彌貧民多利器□□□昏
□□物茲章而盗賊□□是
以□人之言曰我无爲而民自化我好
静而民自正我无事而民自富我欲不
欲而民自樸

adopting for his own use.[65] Could it be that the author, in lines 1–3, is really posing three distinct ways to approach the problem of ruling the empire, only one of which he advocates? That is to say, those lines could be interpreted in this way: "The Confucians, on the one hand, say that we must use the upright and correct to order the state; the Strategists, on the other hand, say we must use surprise tactics when we use troops. But I say that it's only with 'unconcern with affairs' that anyone will take control of the world."

But arguing against this, perhaps, is the fact that *cheng* ("regular," my "upright and correct") and *ch'i* ("irregular," my "surprise tactics") are both part of the planning vocabulary of the Militarists (for example, see Yates, 1988).

[CHAPTER 58]

1 When the government is muddled and confused,
2 The people are genuine and sincere.
3 When the government is discriminate and clear,
4 The **state is crafty and cunning**.

[4a **Disaster is that on which good fortune depends.**]
5 Good fortune is that in which **disaster's** concealed.
6 Who knows where it will end?
7 *For* there is no [fixed] "correct."
8 The "correct" *turns into the "deviant"*;
9 And "good" turns into *"evil."*
10 *People's* state of confusion
11 Has certainly existed for a long time.
12 Therefore be square but don't cut;
13 Be sharp but don't stab;
14 Be straightforward but not unrestrained;
15 Be bright but don't dazzle.

COMMENTS AND NOTES

Text A is like the standard text in adding a line between lines 4 and 5—"Disaster is that on which good fortune depends." Since the chapter concerns the relationship between opposites, the omission of this line in Text B is surely an oversight. Very little survives of Text A: Now missing are lines 1–2 and 6–15.

In the standard text it is again "the people" who are crafty and cunning in line 4.

In other editions of the *Lao-tzu* the last four lines are all said of the Sage: "Therefore, *the Sage* is square but doesn't cut," and so on.

In lines 12–14 the author chooses words that at one and the same time might describe wood and moral traits—"square" (= honest), "sharp" (as an angle = upright), and "straight" (= direct and frank).

[A]

丌正察= 丌

邦夬= 酞∠福之所倚∠福酞之所伏

□□□□□□□□

□□□□□□□□

□□□□□□□□

□□□□□□□□□

[B]

丌正闌= 丌民屯= 丌正察= 丌□□

□福□之所伏孰知丌極□无正也正

□□善復爲□□之恙也丌日固久

矣是以方而不割兼而不剌直而不絏

光而不眺

[CHAPTER 59]

1 For ordering humanity and serving Heaven, nothing's so good as being sparing.

2 For only if you are sparing can you, therefore, early submit [to the Way].

3 Early submission—this is called to repeatedly accumulate *Virtue*.

4 *If you repeatedly accumulate Virtue, then there is nothing you can't overcome.*

5 *When there is nothing you can't overcome*, no one knows *where* it will *end*.

6 *When no one knows where it will end*, you can possess the state.

7 And when you possess the mother of the state, you can last a very long time.

8 This is called [having] deep roots and a firm base,

9 It's the Way of long life and long-lasting vision.

COMMENTS AND NOTES

The first two-thirds of the chapter (lines 1–6) no longer survive in Text A.

The standard text has "this is called" in line 2 where the Ma-wang-tui text has "therefore." So it would read, "Only if you are sparing is this called early submission."

[B]

治人事天莫若嗇夫唯嗇是以蚤■服

■是胃重■積□■

莫■知■亓■

□■之母可□■久是胃□根固氏長生

久視之道也

[A]

□　□　□

□　□　□

□　□　□

□　□　□

□　□　可以有■國

■之母可以長久是胃深槿固氏長□

□■道也

[147]

[CHAPTER 60]

1 Ruling a large state is like cooking small fish.

2 When you use the Way to govern the world, evil spirits won't have godlike power.

3 Actually, it's not that evil spirits won't have godlike power,

4 It's that their power will not harm men.

5 But it's not [just] that <u>their</u> power won't harm men,

6 **The Sage, also**, will not harm them.

7 Since these two do **not** harm others,

8 Therefore their Virtues intermingle and return to them.

COMMENTS AND NOTES

Texts A and B are the same.

Kuei, my "evil spirits," in popular religion are the "ghosts," the souls of people who have died without descendants to provide for them, or the souls of people who have died untimely, sometimes violent, deaths. They cause all sorts of problems for the living.

In line 6 the standard text has "The Sage also will not harm *men*." The Ma-wang-tui variant of "not harm them" *(fu-shang)* allows a number of interpretations of the last three lines. To whom does the "them" refer? Does it mean "men"? I think that it does and translate accordingly. But it might also refer back to the evil spirits, the point being that in the ideal state, the evil spirits would cause no harm to people, and the Sage, in like manner, would not do things harmful to these spirits. As a result, there is harmony in this state between spirits and men.

□□□□□□□□天下亓鬼不
神非亓鬼不神也亓神不傷人也非亓
申不傷人也聖人亦弗傷□□□不相
□□德交歸焉

治大國若亨小鮮以道立天下亓鬼不
神非亓鬼不神也亓神不傷人也非亓
神不傷人也□□□弗傷也夫兩□相
傷故德交歸焉

[149]

[CHAPTER 61, *TEXT A*]

1 The large state is like the lower part of a river;
2 It is the female of the world;
3 It is the meeting point of the world.
4 The female constantly overcomes the male with tranquility.[66]
5 Because she **is** tranquil, **therefore** she is fittingly underneath.

6 The large state—**if** it is below the small **state**, then it **takes** over the small state;
7 The small state—if it is below the large state, then it **is** taken over <u>by</u> the large state.
8 Therefore some by being low take over,
9 And some by being low are taken over.

10 **Therefore** the large state merely desires to unite and rear others;
11 While the small state merely desires to enter and serve others.
12 If both get what they want,
13 **Then the large** *state* **should fittingly** be underneath.

COMMENTS AND NOTES

Text B is like the standard text in having a "therefore" at the start of line 6, and in line 10, Text B has "make stand side by side" *(ping)* in place of "unite" *(chien)*. Text B, as with most other editions of the text, omits the word "state" from the last line.

The Ma-wang-tui version of this chapter differs significantly from what we find in the standard version of the text. To begin with, lines 2 and 3 are reversed, and line 4 in the Ma-wang-tui texts is grammatically more precise. More importantly, the meaning of line 7 is completely changed by the addition of the particle *yü* (here meaning "by"); the standard text of *Lao-tzu* here has "And if the small state is below the large state, then *it takes over the large state.*" In other words, in the standard version the chapter seems to describe a technique of statecraft that will succeed no matter who uses it—presumably what is being advocated is a crafty device of acting humbler and more lowly than one's opponent and in this way drawing him off guard so that he can be defeated. That the Ma-wang-tui version of the chapter is the correct one is confirmed, however, even in the standard version of the text, in which lines 8 and 9 are the same as here.

[A]

大邦者下流也天下之牝∠天下之郊
也牝恒以靚勝牡爲亓靚□宜爲下
∠大邦□下小□則取小﹦邦﹦以下
大邦則取於大邦故或下以取∠或下
而取□大邦者不過欲兼畜人小邦者
不過欲入事人∠夫皆得亓欲∠□□
□□□爲下

[B]

大國□□□□□牝也天下之交
也牝恒以靜朕牡爲亓靜也故宜爲下
也故大國以下□國則取小﹦國﹦以
下大國則取於大國故或下□□□下
而取故大國者不□欲並畜人小國不
□欲入事人夫□亓欲則大者宜爲
下

If the chapter is not about devious statecraft, then there is no need to translate *chien* and *ch'u* in line 10 as "annex and herd others"[67]—the words can mean good things—"unite and rear." And in this way, what had appeared to be a bit of crafty advice now appears to be an appeal to the rulers of large states not to lord it over the small states they want to incorporate; they will be more successful by taking a humble approach.[68]

1 **The Way** is that toward which all things flow.
2 It is the treasure of the good man,
3 And that which protects the bad.

4 Beautiful words can be bought and sold;
5 Honored deeds can be presented to others as gifts;
6 [Even with] things that people regard as no good—will **they** be rejected?
7 Therefore, when the Son of Heaven is being enthroned or the Three Ministers installed,
8 Though you might salute them with disks of jade preceded by teams of four horses,
9 That's not so good as sitting still and offering this.
10 The reason why the ancients valued this—what was it?
11 Did they not say, "Those who seek, **with this** will attain, and those who commit offenses, with this will escape" ?!
12 Therefore, it's the most valued thing in the world.

COMMENTS AND NOTES

Texts A and B are the same: most of line 10 is now missing in Text B.

In line 1 the standard text has "storehouse" or "treasured corner" *(ao)* where the Ma-wang-tui texts have "tendency" or "the way things flow" *(chu)*.[69] And in line 5 the standard text has "add on to" *(chia)* where the Ma-wang-tui texts have "present as a gift" *(ho)*.

In line 7 the standard text has "Three Dukes" *(san-kung)* where the Ma-wang-tui texts have "Three Ministers" *(san-ch'ing)*. On the latter title Hucker has—referring to the meaning of this title during the Chou—a "collective reference to the three eminent officials at the royal court entitled Minister of Education *(ssu-t'u)*, of War *(ssu-ma)*, and of Works *(ssu-k'ung)*."[70] The "Three Dukes" were "ordinarily Grand Preceptor *(t'ai-shih)*, Grand Mentor *(t'ai-fu)*, and Grand Guardian *(t'ai-pao)*."[71] It seems likely that the change from *san-ch'ing* to *san-kung* was made during the Han, when that title assumed greater importance.[72]

Finally, in line 9, the standard texts add the word "Way" at the end; that is, "That's not so good as sitting still and offering this Way."

My interpretation of line 6 is, so far as I can tell, somewhat

[B]

道者萬物之注也善人之珠也不善人
之所保也美言可以市尊行可以賀人
二之不善何□□□□立天子置三鄉
雖有□□璧以先四馬不若坐而進此
古□□□□□□□□不胃求以得
有罪以免與故爲天子貴

[A]

□者萬物之注也善人之珠也不善人
之所珠也美言可以市尊行可以賀
人二之不善也何棄□有乀故立天子
置三卿乀雖有共之璧以先四馬不善
坐而進此古之所以貴此者何也不胃
□□得有罪以免與故爲天下貴

unique. But the thrust of lines 4–6 seems to be that if all of these
things can be presented to others as gifts, then surely the Tao can be
as well.

[CHAPTER 63, TEXT A]

1 Act without acting;
2 Serve without concern for affairs;
3 Find flavor in what has no flavor.

4 Regard the small as large and the few as many,
5 And repay resentment with kindness.
6 Plan for the difficult while *it is easy*;
7 *Act on the large* **while it's minute**.
8 The most difficult things in the world begin as things that are easy;
9 The largest things in the world arise from the minute.
10 Therefore the Sage, to the end does not strive to do the great,
11 And as a result, he is able *to accomplish the great*;
12 *Those who* **too lightly agree** *will necessarily be trusted by few*;
13 **And those who regard many things as easy** will necessarily [end up] with many difficulties.
14 Therefore, even **the Sage** regards things as difficult,
15 And as a result, in the end he has no difficulty.

COMMENTS AND NOTES

On the Way's lack of flavor (line 3), see below, chapter 35, lines 4 and 5.

Though Text A is not in good shape, Text B is worse. Now missing from Text B are lines 2 to the middle of 7, parts of lines 8 and 9, all of lines 10 and 11, and parts of lines 14 and 15. There is a "period" at the start of line 1 in Text A.

The word "things" *(shih)* in lines 8 and 9 is explicit in other editions of the *Lao-tzu*, while it is simply implied in the Ma-wang-tui texts. Also, the standard text has a "necessarily" *(pi)* in lines 8 and 9 (that is, "necessarily begin as" and "necessarily arise from").

[B]

爲无爲□□□□□□□
□□□□□平其細也天
下之□□易天下之大
□□□□□夫輕若□□
信多易必多難是以耶人
□□□之故□
□□

[A]

・爲无爲∠事无事∠味无未大小多
少報怨以德∠圖難乎□□□□
□天下之難作於易天下之大
於細∠是以聖人冬不爲大故能□
□□必多難∠是
□□人猷難之∠故終於无難

[155]

1   **What is at rest is easy to hold;**
2   *What has not yet given a sign is* **easy to plan for;**
3   *The brittle is easily shattered;*
4   *The minute is easily scattered;*
5   *Act on it before it comes into being;*
6   *Order it before it turns into chaos.*

7   A tree [*so big*] *that it takes both arms to surround* starts out as the tiniest shoot;
8   A nine-story terrace rises up from a basket of dirt.
9   A high place one hundred, one thousand feet high begins from under your feet.

10 Those who act on it ruin it;
11 Those who hold on to it lose it.
12 Therefore the Sage does not act,
13 *And as a result,* **he doesn't ruin** [things];
14 **He does not hold on to** [things],
15 **And as a result, he doesn't lose** [things];
16 In people's handling of affairs, they always ruin things when they're right at the point of completion.
17 Therefore we say, "If you're as careful at the end as you were at the beginning, you'll have no failures."
18 Therefore the Sage desires not to desire and doesn't value goods that are hard to obtain;
19 He learns not to learn and returns to what the masses pass by;
20 He could help all things to be natural, yet he dare not do it.

COMMENTS AND NOTES

There is a "period" at the head of line 1 in Text A. In line 9, Text A has "eight hundred feet" *(pai-jen)* where Text B has "one hundred, one thousand." In line 16, Text A has "right at the point of *completing affairs*" *(ch'eng-shih)* in place of "completion" *(ch'eng)*. And in line 17 in Text A the "we say" is omitted.

In line 7 the standard text has "grows from" *(sheng)* instead of "starts out as" *(tso)*. In line 8 in the standard text the terrace rises up from "a pile of " *(lei)* dirt, while in the Ma-wang-tui text the word is "basket" (also *lei*).[73]

Of greater importance, line 9 in most editions of the text is "The journey of a thousand *li* starts from where one stands,"[74]

[A]

·亓安也易持也□□□□□□易謀

□□□□□□□□□□□

毫末九成之臺作於羸土百仁之高台

於足□□□□□□□□□

□也□无敗□无執也故无失也民

之從事也恒於亓成事而敗之∠故慎

終若始則□□□□欲不欲

而不貴難得之腸學不學∠而復衆人

之所過∠能輔萬物之自□□弗敢爲

[B]

□□□□□□□□□□□□□

□木作於毫末九成

之臺作於蔂土百千之高始於足下爲

之者敗之執者失之是以耶人无爲□

□□□□□□□□□民之從事

也恒於亓成事而敗之故曰慎冬若始則

无敗事矣是以耶人欲不欲而不貴難

得之貨學不學復衆人之所過能輔萬

物之自然而弗敢爲

---

though the Text A reading of "A high place of eight hundred feet"
is attested in a few editions.[75]

The "it" in "Those who act on it" in line 10 is omitted in other
texts. And the "Therefore" or "Therefore we say" at the start of line
17 does not occur in other texts.

Finally, the meaning of the last line is clarified with the negative
fu ("not——it") in place of *pu* ("not ——"); it seems clear that
the point is that he *could* do this but he knows he dare not because
such "action" would have adverse effects. The standard reading is
rather "Thus he supports all things in their natural state but does not
take any action."[76]

[157]

[CHAPTER 65]

1 Those who practiced the Way in antiquity,
2 Did not use it to enlighten **the people**.
3 **Rather, they used it to make** them **dumb**.
4 Now the reason why people are difficult to rule is because of
   their knowledge;
5 As a result, to use knowledge to rule the state
6 Is thievery of the state;
7 To use ignorance to rule the state
8 Is kindness to the state.
9 One who constantly understands these two,
10 Also [understands] the principle.
11 To constantly understand the principle—
12 This is called Profound Virtue.
13 Profound Virtue is deep, is far-reaching,
14 **And together with** things it returns.
15 Thus we arrive at the Great Accord.

COMMENTS AND NOTES

In line 1, Text A has "Therefore we say" (or "Therefore, it is said
that"—*ku-yüeh*) "those who practice the Way," which seems to sup-
pose a connection between chapters 64 and 65. But this reading is
unattested in other editions, and any connection between chapters 64
and 65 in terms of ideas is tenuous at best.[77] Presumably the intended word is the same "antiquity" *(ku)* that begins Text B.

The word *shan* ("skilled at," "good at") is added to line 1 in the
standard text—that is, it reads "Those who were *good at* practicing
the Way in antiquity."

In line 4 of the standard text, the reason why people are difficult
to rule is that their knowledge is *too great*, or that they know *too much*
(i ch'i chih to).

In lines 5 and 7, the Ma-wang-tui texts literally say, "To use
knowledge to *know* the state" and "To use not-knowledge to *know* the
state," versus the standard reading of "To use knowledge to *rule* the
state," and so on. That is to say, the *chih* that means knowledge is used
in both lines where the standard text has the *chih* that means "to rule."
But one of the meanings of *chih* ("to know") is "to control" *(chu)* or "to
manage" *(wei)*, and this meaning occurs in relation to what one does to
a state. It is in that sense that I understand *chih* in these lines.[78]

[A]

故曰爲道者非以明民也將以愚之也
民之難□也以亓知也故以知□
之賊也以不知＝邦□德也恒知此
兩者亦稽式也恒知稽式此胃玄＝德
＝深矣遠矣與物□矣乃□□

[B]

古之爲道者非以明□□□之也
夫民之難治也以亓知也故以知＝國
＝之賊也以不知＝＝之德也恒知
此兩者亦稽式也恒知稽式是胃玄＝
德＝深矣遠矣□物反也乃至大順

Line 7 in the standard text differs syntactically from what we find in the Ma-wang-tui texts. The standard text says, "To not use knowledge (or "wisdom"—*chih*) . . . ," whereas the Ma-wang-tui texts have "To use not-knowledge . . ." (i.e., "use" and "not" are reversed). And in line 8 the standard text has "Is *good fortune* for the state" *(fu)* instead of "kindness" or "virtue" *(te)*.

The "constantly" *(heng)* in line 9 is not found in the standard text, while the standard text has an additional "then" *(jan-hou)* at the start of line 15 that is omitted in the Ma-wang-tui texts.

Chapter 65, like chapters 3 and 5 below, can be read in two quite different ways in terms of how the Taoist ruler should rule. What do we make of the fact that he rules without using "knowledge"? Does this mean that he deprives people of education, in an attempt to have a populace of vegetables or automatons that will do his work and never question a thing? Or is the point rather that he recognizes that the premium placed on knowledge and wisdom by the Confucians has its bad side? Thus, what he wants to do away with is crafty, self-serving knowledge that does indeed make for bad relations in people.

1 The reason why rivers and oceans are able to be the **kings** of the one hundred valleys **is that** they **are good** at being below them.
2 For this reason they are able to be the kings of the one hundred valleys.

3 Therefore in the Sage's desire to be above the people,
4 He must in his speech be below them.
5 And in his desire to be at the front of the people,
6 He must in his person be behind them.
7 Thus he dwells above, yet the people do not regard him as heavy;
8 And he dwells in front, yet the people do not see him as posing a threat.
9 The whole world delights in his praise and never tires of him.
10 Is it not **because** he is not contentious,
11 That, as a result, no one in the world can contend with him?!

COMMENTS AND NOTES

In Text A, lines 7 and 8 are reversed. Also, the "whole" or "every-one" *(chieh)* in line 9 is omitted in Text A (as it is in the standard text): it just has "the world" *(t'ien-hsia)*.

The standard text omits the words "the Sage's" *(sheng-jen chih)* from line 3 and thus would read, "Therefore, if *one* desires to be above the people." On the other hand, the standard text *does* say that it is *the Sage* who "dwells above," and so on, in lines 7 and 8: "Thus the Sage dwells above, yet the people do not regard him as heavy." An impressive number of texts agree with the Ma-wang-tui texts on these points and do not accord with the standard edition.

In the standard text, lines 10 and 11 form a statement instead of a question. They read, "Because he does not contend, Therefore, no one in the world can contend with him."

[A]

□海之所以能爲百浴王者以亓善下
之是以能爲百浴王是以聖人之欲上
民也必以亓言下之亓欲先□□必以
亓身後之故居前而民弗害也居上而
民弗重也天下樂隼而弗猒也非以亓
无諍與故□□□□□諍

[B]

江海所以能爲百浴□□□亓□下之
也是以能爲百浴王是以耶人之欲上
民也必以亓言下之亓欲先民也必以
亓身後之故居上而民弗重也居前而
民弗害天下皆樂誰而弗猒也不□亓
无爭與故天下莫能與爭

[161]

CHAPTER 80

1 Let the states be small and people few—
2 Bring it about that there are weapons for "tens" and "hundreds," yet let no one use them;
3 Have the people regard death gravely and put migrating far from their minds.
4 Though they might have boats and carriages, no one will ride them;
5 Though they might have armor and spears, no one will display them.
6 Have the people return to knotting cords and using them.

7 They will relish their food,
8 Regard their clothing as beautiful,
9 Delight in their customs,
10 And feel safe and secure in their homes.
11 Neighboring states might overlook one another,
12 And the **sounds** of chickens and dogs might be **overheard**,
13 Yet the people will arrive at old age and death with no comings and goings between them.

COMMENTS AND NOTES

There is a "period" at the start of line 1 in Text A. In line 3, Text A seems to say, "put *seeing off (sung)* far from their minds." And in line 4 in Text A the words "carriages and boats" are reversed. Line 13 is now missing from Text A, as is most of line 6.

There is a military and a nonmilitary interpretation of the "tens" and "hundreds" in line 2, and most translators seem to prefer the latter (for example, Wing-tsit Chan has "Let there be ten times and a hundred times as many utensils."[79]) I am persuaded to read the "tens" and "hundreds" as designations of troops or platoons, and the "utensils" *(ch'i)* as "weapons" *not* because of new evidence in the Ma-wang-tui texts but rather because I find the argument that ties together lines 2 and 5 and 3 and 4 very convincing; that is, the "carriages and boats" would be used by people who want to migrate, and the armor and spears would be used by troops in battle.[80]

In line 3, the standard text has "Have the people regard death gravely and *not* migrate far." The absence of the negative *pu* in the Ma-wang-tui texts might be copy error; but the line makes good

小國寡民使有十百人器而勿用使民
重死而遠徙又周車无所乘之有甲兵
无所陳之使民復結繩而用之甘亓食
美亓服樂亓俗安亓居哭國相望鷄犬
之□□閒民至老死不相往來

·小邦寡民使十百人之器毋用使民
重死而遠送有車周无所乘之有甲兵
无所陳□□□□□用之甘亓食
美亓服樂亓俗安亓居㷼邦相墾雞狗
之聲相閒民□□□□□□□□

---

sense as it stands, since "putting migrating far from their minds" *(yüan-hsi)* nicely parallels "regarding death gravely" *(chung-ssu).*

The "Although"s *(sui)* at the heads of lines 4 and 5 are explicit in the standard text and simply implied in the Ma-wang-tui text, and in the standard text lines 9 and 10 are reversed.

Angus Graham points out that the second half of this chapter (lines 7–13) are cited by Ssu-ma Ch'ien in relation to the times of Shen-nung and might ultimately stem from a "Tiller" source.[81]

[163]

[CHAPTER 81]

1 Sincere words are not showy;
2 Showy words are not sincere.
3 Those who know are not "widely learned";
4 Those "widely learned" do not know.
5 The good do not have a lot;
6 Those with a lot are not good.

7 The Sage accumulates nothing.
8 Having used what he had for others,
9 He has even more.
10 Having given what he had to others,
11 What he has is even greater.
12 Therefore, the Way of Heaven is to benefit and not cause any harm;
13 The Way of Man is to act on behalf of others and not to compete with them.

COMMENTS AND NOTES

Little remains of Text A: portions of lines 3–8. But the "period" at the start of line 7 is clear.

In the standard text, lines 5 and 6 precede lines 3 and 4, and lines 5 and 6 say something else: "A good man does not argue; He who argues is not a good man";[82] i.e., *pu-pien* replaces *pu-to*.

Lines 5 and 6 in the Ma-wang-tui texts *literally* say, "The good are not many; The many are not good." But the connection between lines 1–6 and then 7–13—assuming there is supposed to be one— seems better if we read *pu-to* ("not much," "not many") as though it were *wu-to* ("not have much"). D. C. Lau translates the same way: "He who is good does not have much; he who has much is not good."[83]

The "Therefore" at the head of line 12 is omitted in the standard text.

In line 13, the standard text begins "The Way of the *Sage*" and ends "and [he] does not compete" *(pu-cheng)* rather than the Ma-wang-tui "and does not compete with them" *(fu-cheng)*.

[A]

□□□□□不□□者不博□者不

知善□□者不善・聖人无積□

以爲□□□□□□□□

[B]

信言不美〓言不信知者不博〓者不
知善者不多〓者不善耵人无積既以
爲人己俞有既以予人矣己俞多故天
之道利而不害人之道爲而弗爭

CHAPTER 67

Chapters 67, 68, and 69 should be read together as a unit.

1 The *whole* world says, I'm Great;
2 Great, yet unlike [everyone else].
3 But it's precisely because I'm unlike [everyone else], that I'm therefore able to be Great.
4 Were I like [everyone else], for a long time now I'd have seemed insignificant and small.

5 I constantly have three treasures;
6 Hold on to them and treasure them.
7 The first is compassion;
8 The second is frugality;
9 And the third is not presuming to be at the forefront in the world.
10 Now, it's because I'm compassionate that I therefore can be courageous;
11 And it's because I'm frugal that I therefore can be magnanimous;
12 And it's because I don't presume to be at the forefront in the world that I therefore can be the head of those with complete talent.
13 **Now**, if you abandon this compassion and yet try to be courageous,
14 And if you abandon this frugality and yet try to be magnanimous,
15 And if you abandon this staying behind and yet go to the fore,
16 Then you will die.
17 If with compassion you attack, then you'll win;
18 If you defend, then you'll stand firm.

19 When Heaven's about to establish him,
20 It's as though he surrounds him with the protective wall of compassion.

COMMENTS AND NOTES

In lines 1–4 the author plays on the double meaning of *hsiao*: it means "to be like" (or resemble), but it also means "small." Therefore these lines could also read, "The whole world says that I'm great

天下□胃我大𣲖而不宵夫唯不宵故
能大若宵久矣亓細也夫我恒有三
市而琛之一日茲亓二曰檢三曰不敢
爲天下先夫茲故能勇檢敢能廣不敢
爲天下先故能爲成器長今舍亓茲且
勇舍亓檢且廣舍亓後且先則死矣夫
茲以單則朕以守則固天將建之如以
茲垣之

□□□□夫唯□故不宵∠
□□∠細久矣我恒有三葆之∠一日
茲二曰檢□□□□□□□□
□□□故能廣不敢爲天下先故能爲
成事長∠今舍亓茲且勇∠舍亓後且
先則必死矣夫茲□□則勝以守則固
天將建之女以茲垣之

(= large, *ta*); Great, yet unlike everyone else (= yet not small). But it's precisely because I'm unlike everyone else (= that I'm not small), that I am therefore able to be Great (= large). Were I like everyone else (= were I small), for a long time now I'd have seemed insignificant."[84]

The Text A and Text B versions of this chapter are quite different. Though the characters are now missing for lines 1 and 2 in Text A, one might hazard a guess that they said, "The world says I am Great, as though unlike [everyone else]" (*t'ien-hsia wei wo ta ssu pu-hsiao*). Then lines 3 and 4 seem to say, "Now, it's because I am *Great*, that I'm unlike [everyone else]. Were I like [everyone else], then I'd have seemed insignificant and small for a long time now."

Line 6 is omitted from Text A, except for the final character "them" (*chih*), in what appears to be copyist error.[85] And copyist error would also seem to account for the complete omission of line 14. Finally, line 16 in Text A reads, "Then you will *certainly* die," and in line 12 Text A has ". . . that I therefore can be the head of those who complete all affairs" (i.e., *ch'eng-shih chang* versus *ch'eng-ch'i chang*).[86]

In the standard text, line 1 reads, "The whole world says that *my Way* is Great" (versus "that I am great"): the omission of the word *tao* ("Way") in the Ma-wang-tui texts is unusual but attested in a small number of other editions.[87] Also, in lines 1–2 the standard text does not repeat the word "great" that stands at the head of line 2 and thus lines 1 and 2 here read more like one line; that is, "The whole world says that my Way is great and seems unlike [anything else]." Line 3 is then most like Text A of the Ma-wang-tui texts—"Now, it's because it is Great, that it therefore seems unlike [anything else]." While line 4 is exactly the same as line 4 in Text B—"Were it like [everything else], for a long time now it would have seemed insignificant and small."

Lines 5–18 in the standard text are exactly the same as we find in Text B of the Ma-wang-tui texts except that the "constantly" is omitted from line 5, the word "this" is omitted from lines 13–15, and the "Then" is omitted at the start of line 16.

Finally, in lines 19 and 20 the standard text says, "When Heaven is about to *save* him" (*chiu* instead of *chien* ["establish"]), "with compassion it *protects* him" (*wei* instead of *huan* ["surround with a wall"]).

[CHAPTER 68]

Chapters 67, 68, and 69 should be read together as a unit.

1 Therefore, one who is good at being a warrior doesn't make a show of his might;
2 One who is good in battle doesn't get angry;
3 One who is good at defeating the enemy doesn't engage him.
4 And one who is good at using men places himself below them.
5 This is called the virtue of not competing;
6 This is called [correctly] using men;
7 This is called matching Heaven.
8 It's the high point of the past.

COMMENTS AND NOTES

The "Therefore" at the head of line 1 is omitted in Text A as it is in the standard text, and in line 7 the word "matching" is omitted.

In line 3 the use of the negative *fu* ("not ——— it/him") in place of *pu* ("not ———") once again adds clarity to the text. The standard text with *pu-yü* instead of *fu-yü* should simply read "doesn't engage" where we have "doesn't engage him."

In line 6 the standard text has "This is called *the strength of* using men" (i.e., *chih-li* is added on at the end).

There has been considerable disagreement among scholars on the punctuation of the last two lines. Many feel that the two lines actually form one: for example, D. C. Lau, using the reading in Text A, which omits the word "matching," translates the end of the chapter: "This is known as the limit that is as old as heaven."[88]

I am persuaded that "using men" *(yung-jen)* and "matching Heaven" *(p'ei-t'ien)* are parallel phrases (they rhyme). The final line stands very well on its own.

[B]

故善爲士者不武善單者不怒善朕敵
者弗與善用人者爲之下是胃不爭□
德是胃用人是胃肥天古之極也

[A]

善爲士者不武∠善戰者不怒∠善勝
敵者弗□善用人者爲之下□胃不静
之德是胃用人是胃天古之極也

Chapters 67, 68, and 69 should be read together as a unit.

1 Those who use weapons have a saying which goes:
2 "I don't presume to act like the host, and instead play the part of the guest;
3 I don't advance an inch, but rather retreat a foot."
4 This is called moving forward without moving forward—
5 Rolling up one's sleeves without baring one's arms—
6 Grasping firmly without holding a weapon—
7 And enticing to fight when there's no opponent.
8 Of disasters, none is greater than [thinking] you have no rival.
9 To think you have no rival is to come close to losing my treasures.
10 Therefore, when weapons are raised and [the opponents] are fairly well matched,
11 Then it's the one who feels grief that will win.

COMMENTS AND NOTES

There is a "period" at the start of line 1 in Text A. Text B, like the standard text, omits the "I" at the head of line 3 and parallels line 2 by adding "presume" (Don't presume to advance an inch . . ."). There are two mistakes in Text A that do not occur in Text B: in line 8 the copyist mistakenly wrote down two "thans" *(yü yü)* instead of "greater than" *(ta-yü),* and then in line 9 he mistakenly repeated the "my" *(wu-wu)* of "my treasures." In line 10, Text B accords with later texts in having "when swords (or weapons) are crossed" *(k'ang-ping)* instead of "when weapons are raised" *(ch'eng-ping).*

I read the *hsing wu-hsing* ("going forward without going forward") of line 4 as parallel to *wei wu-wei* ("act without acting") and *shih wu-shih* ("serve without concern for affairs") since the point is that in this way you progress towards victory even though you do not physically advance. If the line is strictly parallel with the lines that follow, then the second *hsing* should be a noun to match with "arms" and "weapons" and "opponent," which would give us something like D. C. Lau's "Marching forward when there is no road,"[89] or Wing-tsit Chan's "To march without formation."[90]

The "those who use weapons" *(yung-ping)* in line 1 refers to the "Strategists" or "Militarists" *(ping-chia)* in early China.

[B]

用兵又言曰吾不敢爲主而爲客不敢
進寸而退尺是胃行无行攘无臂乀執
无兵乃无敵禍莫大於無二敵二近○
亡吾琛矣故抗兵相若而依者朕□

[A]

·用兵有言曰吾不敢爲主而爲客吾
不進寸而芮尺是胃行无行襄无臂執
无兵乃无敵矣蹶莫於於无二適二斤
亡吾葆矣故稱兵相若則哀者勝矣

The "which goes" *(yüeh)* of line 1 is not found in the standard text, and in the standard text, lines 6 and 7 are reversed.

In lines 8 and 9 the standard text has "regarding your rival too lightly" *(ch'ing-ti)* instead of "[thinking] you have no rival" *(wu-ti)*, and in line 10 for "fairly well matched" *(hsiang-jo)* the standard text has "meet one another" *(hsiang-chia)*.

[CHAPTER 70]

1 My words are easy to understand,
2 And easy to put into practice.
3 Yet no one in the world can understand them,
4 And no one can put them into practice.
5 Now my words have an ancestor, and my deeds have a lord,
6 And it's simply because [people] have no understanding [of them], that they therefore don't understand me.
7 But when those who understand me are few, then I'm of great value.
8 Therefore the Sage wears coarse woolen cloth, but inside it he holds on to jade.

COMMENTS AND NOTES

Text A is like the standard text in having *"very* easy to understand" and *"very* easy to put into practice" in lines 1 and 2. In line 3, Text A has "people" *(jen)* instead of "the world" *(t'ien-hsia)*, that is, "And yet of people, no one . . ." In line 5, Text A accords with the standard text in reversing the words "ancestor" and "lord"; it has "My words have a lord, and my deeds have an ancestor."

The Ma-wang-tui version of this chapter, with all of the proper grammatical particles added, is much clearer and more precise than the version found in later texts.[91]

吾言甚易知也甚易行也而人莫之能
知也而莫之能行也言有君∠事有宗
夫唯无知也是以不□□□□□
我貴矣是以聖人被褐而裹玉

吾言易知也易行也而天下莫之能知
也莫之能行也夫言又宗事又君夫唯
无知也是以不我知￢者希則我貴矣
是以耵人被褐而裹玉

[CHAPTER 71]

1   To know you don't know is best.
2   Not to know you [**don't**] know is a flaw.
3   Therefore, the Sage's not **being flawed**
4   Stems from his recognizing a flaw as a flaw.
5   Therefore, he is flawless.

COMMENTS AND NOTES

The "don't" in line 2 occurs in Text A (by virtue of ditto marks) but has been omitted—mistakenly I think—in Text B and all subsequent editions of the *Lao-tzu*. Without it, one is forced to translate the line in the fashion of Wing-tsit Chan: "To pretend to know when you do not know is a disease."[92] D. C. Lau assumes that the Text B reading is still right and translates, "Not to know yet to think that one knows will put one in difficulty."[93] I agree with Wu Fu-hsiang[94] in feeling that the Text A reading—*pu-chih pu-chih* (literally "not know not know")—represents the original text (versus the standard reading of *pu-chih chih*—literally "not know know").

Although *ping* in lines 2–5 does mean "disease" (Chan and Waley; Lau has "difficulty"), here it is best translated, I feel, as "flaw" (or "fault" or "defect").

The standard text adds a line between lines 2 and 3: Chan's translation of that line reads, "Only when one recognizes this disease as a disease can one be free from the disease."

The standard text then omits the "Therefore" at the head of line 3 and omits the possessive particle following "the Sage," destroying the dependent relationship of lines 3 and 4. Chan's translation of lines 3–5 in the standard text reads, "The sage is free from the disease. Because he recognizes this disease to be disease, he is free from it."

[B]

知不知尚矣不知〓病矣是以耶人之
不□也以元病〓也是以不病

[A]

知不知尚矣〵不〓知〓病矣是以聖
人之不病〻以元□□□□□□

[CHAPTER 72]

1 When the people don't respect those in power, then what they greatly fear is about to arrive.

2 Don't narrow the size of the places in which they live;
3 Don't oppress them in their means of livelihood.
4 It's simply because you do not oppress them, that they therefore will not be fed up.
5 Therefore the Sage knows himself but doesn't show himself;
6 He cherishes himself but doesn't value himself.
7 For this reason, he rejects that and takes this.

COMMENTS AND NOTES

Most of lines 1, 5, and 6 are now missing in Text A. Line 2 in Text A is set off from line 1 with a "period."

The differences between the Ma-wang-tui version of this chapter and that of the standard text are largely grammatical. In line 1 the word "about to" *(chiang)* does not occur in the standard text. In lines 2 and 3, the Ma-wang-tui texts use the imperative negative *(wu)* instead of the regular *wu* in the standard text. In line 4, "do not oppress them" is formed with the negative *fu* (not ——— them) instead of *pu* (not ———).

In two places in the chapter the author plays on multiple meanings of words. In line 1 the word *wei* (to " fear," "stand in awe of," "respect," "dread," but also the "awesome," "powerful," "authority") is used three different times: the line literally says, "When the people do not *wei wei*, then the great *wei* is about to arrive." Then in line 4, the text literally says, "It's simply because you do not *yen* (oppress) them, that they therefore will not be *yen* (here meaning 'fed up')."

民之不畏= 則大畏將至矣毋伸亓所
居毋猒亓所生夫唯弗猒是以不猒是
以耵人自知而不自見也自愛而不自
貴也故去罷而取此

□□□畏= 則大□□□矣‧母閒亓
所居毋猒亓所生夫唯弗猒是□□□
自貴也故去被取此□□□□□□而不

[CHAPTER 73]

1 If you're brave in being daring, you'll be killed;
2 If you're brave in not being daring, you'll live.
3 *With these* two things, in one case there's profit, in the other there's harm.
4 The things Heaven hates—who knows why?
5 The Way of Heaven is not to fight yet to be good at winning—
6 Not to speak yet skillfully respond—
7 No one summons it, yet it comes on its own—
8 To be at ease yet carefully plan.
9 Heaven's net is large and vast;
10 Its mesh may be coarse yet nothing slips through.

COMMENTS AND NOTES

There is a "period" at the start of line 1 in Text A.

With the addition of the nominalizing particle *che*, lines 1 and 2 in Text A read, "The *one who is* brave in being daring will be killed. The *one who is* brave in not being daring will live." Line 7 in Text A is like line 7 in the standard text: it reads, "Not to be summoned yet come on its own" (that is, it has the negative *pu* instead of *fu*). This is better than the reading in B in that it involves no change in subject from lines 5–8. All that remains of this chapter in Text A are lines 6–8, part of line 1, and most of line 2.

A line is added between lines 4 and 5 in the standard text: "Therefore even the Sage finds it difficult." And in line 5, the standard text has "compete" instead of "fight" in the phrase "not to fight yet be good at winning."

[B]

勇於敢則殺勇於不敢則栝□兩者或
利或害天之所亞孰知亓故天之道不
單而善朕不言而善應弗召而自來單
而善謀天罔祏 [二] 疏而不失

[A]

· 勇於敢者□□於不敢者則栝□

□□□□ ∠不言而善應∠

不召而自來彈而善謀□□□□□□

□
□

CHAPTER 74

1 If the people were constant [in their behavior] and yet did not fear death,

2 How could you use execution to intimidate them?

3 If you brought it about that the people were constant [in their behavior] and moreover feared death, and [we] took those who behaved in abnormal ways and killed them—who would dare act in this way?!

4 If the people are constant and moreover necessarily fear death, then we constantly have the one in charge of executions.

5 Now killing people in place of the one in charge of executions, this [is like] cutting wood in place of the head carpenter.

6 And of those who cut wood in place of the head carpenter, very few do not hurt their hands!

COMMENTS AND NOTES

In line 1 in Text B the copyist mistakenly added a "fear" *(wei)* before the "did not fear" *(pu-wei)*: I leave this out in the translation. The first part of line 3 is different in Text A from what we find in Text B, but it makes no sense and the copyist's mistakes can be reconstructed.[95] Text A is like the standard text in line 3 in saying, "and *we* took those who behaved in abnormal ways." This "we" *(wu)* seems not to occur in Text B (if we are right in assuming that the missing character at this point is *chiang* ["would"]).

The Ma-wang-tui texts differ from all later editions of the *Lao-tzu* in having a *ch'ieh* ("and yet," "and moreover") between "constantly" and "fear" in lines 1, 3, and 4. That is to say, in most later texts the phrase is "constantly did not fear" in line 1 and "constantly feared" in line 3 (the first part of line 4 does not occur in later editions). Most scholars working on the Ma-wang-tui texts of the *Lao-tzu* seem to ignore this *ch'ieh* and treat these lines as if it were not there (e.g., D. C. Lau translates the relevant lines, "If the common people are constantly unafraid of death," "If the people were constantly afraid of death," and "If the people are constantly afraid of death"[96]). I prefer to read the *ch'ieh* in its normal grammatical way, and I think that "constant behavior" is meant to contrast with the "behaving in abnormal ways" *(wei-ch'i)* brought up in line 3. Note that Lao-tzu feels that people should (or naturally do) fear death; at

[181]

[A]

□□□□□□□奈何以殺愳之也若

民恒是死則而爲者吾將得而殺之∠

夫孰敢矣若民□□必畏死則恒有司

殺者夫伐司殺者殺∠是伐大匠斲也

夫伐大匠斲者則□不傷亓手矣

[B]

若民恒且○不畏死若以殺瞿之也

使民恒且畏死而爲畸者□得而殺之

夫孰敢矣若民恒且必畏死則恒又司

殺者夫代司殺者殺是代大匠斲夫代

大匠斲則希不傷亓手

---

present they do not because their lives are being made so miserable by their rulers (on this point see the next chapter).

The "If" *(jo)* at the head of line 1 does not occur in later editions; hence the first line of the chapter is often translated as a firm statement (e.g., Chan has "The people are not afraid of death"[97]). Also in line 2, the standard text has "death" *(ssu)* in place of "execution" (or "killing"—*sha*).

Line 4 in the standard text simply reads, "We constantly have the one in charge of executions to do the killing." (Note that the phrase "to do the killing" is not tacked on to this line in the Mawang-tui texts.) The "one in charge of executions" here is normally understood to be Heaven or "Nature"; that is, the good ruler will let death occur naturally to his people and not execute them at will.

In line 5 the standard text says, "this is called cutting wood . . ." *(shih-wei)* instead of "this [is like] cutting wood . . ." *(shih)*.

Finally, in the last line the standard text says something like "in a very *few cases will there be* those who do not hurt their hands" *(hsi-yu)* versus the Ma-wang-tui reading of "*very few* do not hurt their hands" *(hsi)*.

[CHAPTER 75]

1 The reason why people starve,
2 Is because they take so much in tax-grain.
3 Therefore they starve.
4 The reason why the common people cannot be ruled,
5 Is because their superiors have their reasons for acting.
6 **Therefore** they cannot be ruled.

7 The reason why people take death lightly,
8 Is because they so avidly seek after life.
9 Therefore they take death lightly.
10 Only those who do not act for the purpose of living—
11 Only these are superior to those who value life.

COMMENTS AND NOTES

Texts A and B are essentially the same. There is a "period" at the start of line 1 in Text A and also at the start of line 7.

In the standard text lines 2 and 8 agree with line 5 in saying "their superiors" *(ch'i-shang)* instead of just "they" *(ch'i)*; this is no doubt implied in the Ma-wang-tui texts, but the meaning could be confusing—it is not readily apparent who the "they" are in lines 2 and 8.

The word "take" *(ch'ü)* is omitted in line 2 in the standard text and simply implied.

In lines 4 and 6 the standard text has "The reason why the people are *difficult to rule* (or order)" *(nan-chih)* instead of "cannot be ruled (or brought into order)" *(pu-chih)*.

In line 5 in the standard text the word "reasons" is omitted in the phrase "have their reasons for acting" *(yu i-wei)* and the phrase would be better translated as "have actions" or "take action."

Finally, the last two lines are somewhat awkward grammatically in Chinese with a change in subject (in the Ma-wang-tui texts as well as later texts). Literally they say, "Only those who do not act with living in mind, Only *this* is worth more than valuing life."

人之飢也以亓取食貌之多是以飢百
生之不治也以亓上之有以爲也□以
不治民之輕死也以亓求生之厚也是
輕死夫唯无以生爲者是賢貴生

・人之飢也以亓取食逃之多也是以
飢百姓之不治也以亓上有以爲□是
以不治・民之坙死以亓求生之厚也
是以坙死夫唯无以生爲者是賢貴生

1 When people are born, they're supple and soft;
2 When they die, they end up stretched out firm and rigid;[98]
3 When the ten thousand things and grasses and trees are alive,
   they're supple and pliant;
4 When they're dead, they're withered and dried out.
5 Therefore we say that the firm and rigid are companions of
   death,
6 While the supple, the soft, the weak, and the delicate are
   companions of life.
7 If a soldier is rigid, he won't win;
8 If a tree is rigid, it will come to its end.
9 Rigidity and power occupy the inferior position;
10 Suppleness, softness, weakness, and delicateness occupy the
   superior position.

COMMENTS AND NOTES

There is a "period" at the start of line 1 in Text A.

Text B is like the standard text in omitting the words "weak and delicate" *(wei-hsi)* in lines 6 and 10. Text B agrees with the standard text in having "Therefore" *(shih-i)* at the head of line 7. Text B also has a "Therefore" *(ku)* at the start of line 9.

At the end of line 8, Text B has *ching* (normally "compete") where Text A has "end up" or "come to its end" (as in line 2, reading *heng* as *keng*), while the Wang Pi text has "it will be used as a weapon" *(ping)* and most texts say, curiously, "it will work together" *(kung)*. The variant that makes the most sense here is one that occurs in just a few texts, *che* ("broken"); i.e., "If a tree is rigid it will be broken" (as in a storm). Chou Tz'u-chi makes the plausible suggestion of reading the *ching* in Text B to mean "strong" but also "lying down stiffly" (as in death).[99]

In line 2 in the standard text, the words "end up stretched out" do not occur. And at the head of line 5, the standard text simply says "Therefore" *(ku)* instead of "Therefore we say" *(ku-yüeh)*.

[B]

人之生也柔弱亓死也㤹信堅强萬□
□木之生也柔椊亓死也椁槀故曰堅
强死之徒也柔弱生之徒也□以兵强
則不朕木强則兢故强大居下柔弱居
上

[A]

・人之生也柔弱亓死也蓎仞賢∠
萬物草木之生也柔脆亓死也椁蕶∠
故曰堅强者死之徒也柔弱微細∠生
之徒也兵强則不勝木强則恒∠强大
居下∠柔弱微細居上

CHAPTER 77

1 The Way of Heaven is like the flexing of a bow.
2 The high it presses down; the low it raises up.
3 From those with a surplus it takes away; to those without enough it **adds on**.
4 **Therefore the Way of Heaven—**
5 Is to reduce the excessive and increase the insufficient;
6 The Way of Man—
7 Is to reduce the insufficient and offer more to the excessive.
8 Now, who is able to have a surplus **and use it** to offer to Heaven?[100]
9 Clearly, it's only the one who possesses the Way.
10 Therefore the Sage—
11 Takes actions but does not possess them;
12 Accomplishes his tasks but does not dwell on them.
13 Like this, is his desire not to make a display of his worthiness.

COMMENTS AND NOTES

Line 1 in Text A has "the world" *(t'ien-hsia)* where Text B has "Heaven" *(t'ien)*, but I think this is a mistake.[101] Text A is like the standard text in line 6 in adding the words "then is not so" (or "is not like this"—*tse pu-jan*). Only about one-half of Text A now remains; missing are portions of lines 1, 5, 6, 7, and 13, and all of lines 10, 11, and 12.

The "Therefore" at the start of line 4 does not occur in the standard text. Instead of "increase" *(i)* in line 5, the standard text has "add on to" or "supplement" *(pu,* as at the end of line 3), and in place of the "and" *(erh)* in line 7 the standard text has "in order to" *(i)*.

At the end of line 8 all other known editions of the *Lao-tzu* have "offer it to the world" *(feng t'ien-hsia* where the Ma-wang-tui texts have "offer to Heaven." The variant "world" on the surface seems better, though the Ma-wang-tui line also makes sense. The Ma-wang-tui copyists may have mistakenly omitted the *hsia* after the *t'ien.* It also seems possible that the correct word was *wu* ("not have," "those without"—the two characters look much alike) in which case the line would read, "Now, who is able to have a surplus and take it to offer to those who have nothing? "

Line 11 in the standard text is "Takes actions but does not *rely*

[A]

□見賢也

□□□
□□□
□□□
以取奉於天者乎
不祭敗□□奉有餘孰能有餘而有
故天之道敗有□□□奉有餘
者舉之有餘者敗之∠不足者補之∠
天下□□□者也高者印之下

[B]

弗居也若此亓不欲見賢也
又道者乎是以耶人爲而弗又成功而
又余夫孰能又余而□■奉於天者唯
云有余而益人之道云不足者奉
有余者云之不足者□□
天之道酉張弓也高者印之下者舉之

[on them]" (*pu-shih* instead of *fu-yu*). Line 12 begins, "His tasks are accomplished" (*kung-ch'eng* instead of *ch'eng-kung*—on which see chapter 17, below). And the words "Like this" are omitted from the head of line 13.

CHAPTER 78

1 In the whole world, nothing is softer and weaker than water.
2 *And yet for attacking* **the hard and strong, nothing can** *beat* **it,**
3 Because there is nothing you can use to replace it.
4 That water can defeat the unyielding—
5 That the weak can defeat the strong—
6 There is no one in the whole world who doesn't know it,
7 And yet *there is no one who can* **put** *it* **into practice.**
8 For this reason, the words of the Sage say:
9 To take on yourself the disgrace of the state—this is called being the lord of [the altars of] earth and grain;
10 To assume responsibility for all ill-omened events in the state— this is called being the king of the world.
11 Correct words seem to say the reverse [of what you expect them to say].

COMMENTS AND NOTES

Each state in early China had its "altars of earth and grain" where sacrifices to agricultural deities took place; hence any state ruler was a "lord of the altars of earth and grain."

What remains of Text A seems to indicate that Texts A and B were exactly the same in the case of this chapter, with the exception of some insignificant grammatical changes. Parts of lines 1, 2, 4, 5, 6, and 7 are now missing from Text A.

Lines 4 and 5 are reversed in the standard text, and for "water" in line 4 the standard text has "the soft."

The "And yet" *(erh)* at the head of line 7 is not found in the standard text, but it is an attested variant.[102]

For line 8, the standard text has "Therefore the Sage says" (rather than "the words of the Sage" *sheng-jen chih yen*—also a known variant). The Ma-wang-tui reading is superior since the "correctness" of these "words" is noted in the last line.[103]

Finally, in line 10 the standard text has "this is to be" *(shih wei)* instead of "this is called" *(shih wei)*, but "this is called" is a common variant in this line.[104]

天下莫柔弱於水□□□□□
□以亓無以易之也水之朕剛也弱之
朕強也天下莫弗知也而□□□□也
是故耶人之言云曰受國之訽是胃社
稷之主受國之不祥是胃天下之王正
言若反

乙
天下莫柔□□□□□堅強者莫之能
□也以亓无□易□□□□□勝
強乙天□□□□□行也故聖人
之言云乙曰受邦之訽是胃社稷之主
受邦之不祥是胃天下之王□□若反

[CHAPTER 79, *TEXT A*]

1 To make peace where there has been great resentment, there is bound to be resentment left over.
2 How could this be regarded as good?
3 Therefore the Sage [**holds**] the right tally yet makes no demands of others.
4 For this reason, those who have virtue are in charge of the tally;
5 **Those without** virtue are in charge of the taxes.
6 The Way of Heaven has no favorites,
7 It's always with the good man.

[7a **Virtue—3,041 (characters)**]

COMMENTS AND NOTES

Line 7a is found only at the end of Text B. Text B is like the standard text in having the word "holds" *(chih)* in line 3; the word is simply implied in Text A. Also, Text B is like the standard text in saying "the left tally" where Text A has "the right," the right and left tallies being two halves of a contract that has been split in two, one half being kept by the buyer, and one half by the seller.

The Text A reading of "right tally" in line 3 is significant since the general practice in ancient China was for the superior partner in a contractual arrangement to hold on to the *right* portion of the contract while the inferior partner held on to the left. That the Sage according to Lao-tzu kept the "left" portion (the reading in the standard text and in Text B) has been understood in two different and contrasting ways, one being that Lao-tzu says in chapter 31 that in auspicious affairs the "left" is superior while in affairs of mourning the superior is the "right" (so the Sage here would be in the superior role), the other being that Lao-tzu here as elsewhere naturally puts the Sage in the inferior position. (The argument is also made that for people of Ch'u, in contrast to people in other parts of China, the left was the superior position as opposed to the right.[105])

My own feeling is that the point being made is that even though the Sage is in the superior role and all others owe a lot to him, he makes no demands on others, never asking them to live up to their part of the bargain, and in this way causes no resentment. Therefore I feel that "right" here in Text A is the right word.[106]

The "Therefore" at the head of line 4 does not occur in the standard text, but it is a common variant.

和大怨必有餘怨∠焉可以為善是以

聖右介而不以責於人故有德司介□

德司彻夫天道无親恒與善人

禾大□□□□□□□為善是以耵

人執左芥而不以責於人故又德司芥

无德司彻□□□□□□□□

三千卌一　　　　　　　　　　德

The "taxes" in line 5 *(ch'e)* refer to taxes in tithe. Those without virtue, in contrast to the Sage, will indeed insist that the people pay up.

Text B indicates a total of 3,041 characters in this part of the text and 2,426 characters in the *Tao* part that will follow. Thus we assume that when the text was fully preserved, Ma-wang-tui Text B had a total of 5,467 characters. The present Wang Pi text of *Lao-tzu* has only 5,268 characters and the present Ho-shang Kung, 5,281. But Hsieh Shou-hao's *Hun-yüan sheng-chi* (completed in 1191) preserves the words of Fu I (A.D. 554–639), where he claims he had available to him versions of the text with 5,722, 5,635, 5,683, and 5,555 characters. (For more on this point, see Henricks, 1985, p. 31.)

TAO

(THE WAY)

1 As for the Way, the Way that can be spoken of is not the constant Way;
2 As for names, the name that can be named is not the constant name.
3 The nameless is the beginning of the ten thousand things;
4 The named is the mother of the ten thousand things.

5 **Therefore**, those constantly without desires, by this means will perceive its subtlety.
6 Those constantly with desires, by this means will see only that which they yearn for and seek.

7 These two together emerge;
8 They have different names yet they're called the same;
9 That which is even more profound than the profound—
10 The **gateway** of all subtleties.

COMMENTS AND NOTES

There is a "period" at the start of line 1 in Text A.

Though there is a lacuna at the beginning of line 5 in Text A, the "therefore" occurs here in Text B, and there seems no reason to doubt that it originally occurred here in Text A as well. The same is true for "gateway" *(men)* in the last line. The second part of line 1 and the first part of line 2 are missing from Text B; so, too, is the second part of line 5. For the rest, Text B is exactly the same as Text A with the exception of a few variant characters, homophones that do not affect the meaning.

The grammatical form of lines 1 and 2 in the Ma-wang-tui texts differs from that of the standard text, that difference resulting in the additional phrase at the start of each line—"As for the Way" and "As for names."[107]

Note that in the Ma-wang-tui texts in line 3, the nameless is the beginning of the "ten thousand things," not "Heaven and Earth," as most texts have it.

Line 6 in the standard text has "Those constantly with desires, by this means see *ch'i-chiao,*" its "boundaries" (or "outcomes"). The Ma-wang-tui texts add the particle *so* ("that which") to this phrase— that is, they have *ch'i so-chiao,* and the *chiao* used is a different character, one that means "to cry" or "to wail." The particle *so* requires

[A]

・道可道也∠非恒道也∠名可名也
非恒名也无名萬物之始也∠有名萬
物之母也□恒无欲也以觀其眇∠恒
有欲也以觀其所噭兩者同出異名同
胃玄之有玄眾眇之□

[B]

道可道□□□□□□恒名也
无名萬物之始也有名萬物之母也故
恒无欲也□□□□恒又欲也以觀
所噭兩者同出異名同胃玄之又玄眾
眇之門

a verb to follow it, and the character that means "border" as a noun means "to seek" or "desire" as a verb, and this is the reading I use.[108] Also on this line, the word "only" is not found here in the Chinese, and some read lines 5 and 6 as both positive things the Taoist should do (i.e., he sees things completely only by both having and not having desires). I find that position untenable given all that Lao-tzu says about desires and the need to lessen them or eliminate them in the rest of the book.

The possibility of punctuating the text in such a way that "nonbeing" (*wu*) and "being" (*yu*) would be the focus of lines 5 and 6 instead of "without desires" (*wu-yŭ*) and "having desires" (*yu-yŭ*)—Wing-tsit Chan, for example, has "Therefore let there always be nonbeing, so we may see their subtlety, And let there always be being, so we may see their outcome"[109]—seems precluded in the Ma-wang-tui texts by the fact that *wu-yŭ* and *yu-yŭ* are grammatically set off for emphasis.

The end of the chapter is worded somewhat differently in the Ma-wang-tui texts than it is elsewhere—here we clearly seem to have four four-character lines.

CHAPTER 2

1 When everyone in the world knows the beautiful as beautiful,
    ugliness comes into being;

2 When everyone knows the good, then the not good comes to be.

3 **The mutual** production **of being and nonbeing,**

4 The mutual completion of difficult and easy,

5 The mutual formation of long and short,

6 The mutual filling of high and low,

7 The mutual harmony of tone and voice,

8 The mutual following of front and back—

9 These are all constants.[110]

10 Therefore the Sage dwells in nonactive affairs and practices the
    wordless teaching.

11 The ten thousand things arise, but he doesn't begin them;

12 He acts on their behalf, but he doesn't make them dependent;

13 He accomplishes his tasks, but he doesn't dwell on them;

14 It is only because he doesn't dwell on them, that they therefore
    do not leave him.

COMMENTS AND NOTES

Line 1 in Text A is not exactly the same: the difference might be
translated as "When everyone in the world knows the beautiful *is*
beautiful . . ."—in any event, the difference is slight *(mei wei mei* instead of *mei chih wei mei).* Missing from Text A are the words from
"practices" in line 10 to the end of the next line. Text A omits the
negative in the last line, giving "Just because he dwells on them,
therefore . . ." That must be scribal error, since the line makes little
sense in this way.

    In line 7 Text A has "the mutual harmony of *idea* and voice"
(*i* instead of *yin*)—an intriguing variation. Nonetheless, it is not certain that the copyist did not mean "tone" here even though he wrote
"idea," that is, the character meaning "idea" might be an abbrevia-
tion of or a loan for the character that means "tone."

    In contrast to the standard *Lao-tzu* text, the Ma-wang-tui texts
in line 2 simply say, "When everyone knows the good," not "When
everyone knows the good as good." More important is the change to
lines 3–9. In the standard text this is a series of statements: "Being
and nonbeing produce one another; difficult and easy complete one
another," and so on. Here these lines seem to form a series of nom-

[A]

天下皆知美爲美惡已乚皆知善訧不
善乚矣乚有无之相生也難易之相成
也長短之相刑也高下之相盈也乚意
聲之相和也先後之相隋恒也是以聲
人居无爲之事行□□□□□□□□
□□也爲而弗志也成功而弗居也乚
夫唯居是以弗去

[B]

天下皆知美之爲美亞已皆知善斯不
善矣□□□□生也難易之相成也長
短之相刑也高下之相盈也音聲之相
和也先後之相隋恒也是以耵人居无
爲之事行不言之教萬物昔而弗始爲
而弗侍也成功而弗居也夫唯弗居是
以弗去

inal phrases that are only defined in line 9 ("These are all constants."). Line 9 does not occur in any other text of the *Lao-tzu*. Equally valid grammatically would be the reading "Being is the thing mutually produced by nonbeing, Difficult is the thing mutually produced by easy ... These are all constants."[111]

Note that in the Ma-wang-tui texts, in line 5, long and short mutually "form" (*hsing*) one another—they do not "compare" or "contrast" (*chiao*) one another (*hsing* is a known variant here). And in line 6, high and low mutually "fill" (*ying*) one another, they do not "overturn" (*ch'ing*) one another. Note, too, that the Ma-wang-tui texts omit the line found in some texts of *Lao-tzu* between lines 11 and 12—"He produces them, but he doesn't own them" (or "They are produced, but he doesn't own them"—*sheng erh pu-yu*).

In lines 12 and 13 I think the subject shifts from the "ten thousand things" of line 11 back to "the Sage" of line 10, and thus what is said here of the Sage parallels what is said of the Tao in lines 7–9 of chapter 51. Strictly speaking, the subject should remain the "ten thousand things." If that is the author's intent, then we should best translate lines 12 and 13, "They act, but he doesn't make them dependent; They accomplish their tasks but he doesn't dwell on them."

[CHAPTER 3]

1   By not elevating the worthy, you bring it about that people will not compete.

2   By not valuing goods that are hard to obtain, you bring it about that people will not act like thieves.

3   By not displaying the desirable you bring it about that people will not be confused.

4   Therefore, in the government of the Sage:

5   He empties their minds,

6   And fills their bellies.

7   Weakens their ambition,

8   And strengthens their bones.

9   He constantly causes the people to be without knowledge and without desires.

10   If he can bring it about that those with knowledge simply do not dare to act,

11   Then there is nothing that will not be in order.

COMMENTS AND NOTES

What survives of Text A (the first part of line 1, the second part of line 2, parts of lines 3 and 4, lines 8 and 9) is word-for-word the same as Text B.

The only appreciable differences between the Ma-wang-tui texts and other editions of the *Lao-tzu* occur in lines 3 and 10. Most texts of *Lao-tzu* have "bring it about that people's *minds* will not be confused" in line 3, and in line 10 the standard *Lao-tzu* text has "He causes the knowledgeable to not dare to act. If he acts without action *(wei wu-wei)*, then there is nothing that will not be in order."[112]

[B]

不上賢使民不爭不貴難得之貨使民
不爲盜不見可欲使民不亂是以耶人
之治也虛亓心實亓腹弱亓志強亓骨
恒使民无知无欲也使夫知不敢弗爲
而已則无不治矣

[A]

不上賢□　　民
不爲□不□　□民
□民不瓜乚是以聲
人之□□強其
骨恒使民无知无欲也使□
□□□□□□□□□□□

[CHAPTER 4]

1 The Way is empty;
2 Yet when you use it, you never need fill it again.
3 Like an abyss! It seems to be the ancestor of the ten thousand
   things.

4 It files down sharp edges;
5 Unties the tangles;
6 Softens the glare;
7 And settles the dust.

8 Submerged! It seems perhaps to exist.
9 We don't know whose child it is;
10 It seems to have [even] preceded the Lord.

COMMENTS AND NOTES

Parts of lines 1, 2, and 7 are missing from Text A. Text A has the
synonym *hsiao* ("deep and still") for *yüan* ("abyss") in line 3, and the
jui ("sharp edges") is omitted in line 4 through—one assumes—copy
error.

This chapter varies very little from the standard *Lao-tzu* form.
The *yu* ("again") for *huo* ("perhaps") in line 2 is a known variant,
and the *ts'o* ("file down") for *ts'o* ("press down") would appear to be
the right word. The Ma-wang-tui texts have *ying* ("fill") instead of
man ("fill") at the end of line 2. The change to *man* in later editions
was one of a number of substitutions made to avoid the personal
name of an emperor, in this case the name of Emperor Hui of the
Han (r. 194–187 B.C.), Liu Ying.[113]

"Lord" (Ti) was the name of the supreme deity of the Shang
people (traditional dates 1766–1122 B.C.); Ti was also used as a name
for the supreme god of the Chou (1122–221 B.C.), though they more
commonly used the name "Heaven" (T'ien).

[A]

□□□□□盈也乚　瀟呵始萬物
□之宗乚　銼其乚　解其紛乚　和其光同□
□□□或存乚　吾不知□子也乚　象
帝之先乚

[B]

道沖而用之有弗盈也淵呵佁萬物之
宗銼亓兌解亓芬和亓光同亓䣮湛呵
佁或存吾不知亓誰之子也象帝之先

[CHAPTER 5]

1 Heaven and Earth are not humane;
2 They regard the ten thousand things as straw dogs.
3 The Sage is not humane;
4 He **regards** the common people as straw dogs.

5 The space between Heaven and Earth—is it not like a bellows?
6 It is empty and yet not depleted;
7 Move it and more [always] comes out.
8 Much learning means frequent exhaustion.
9 That's not so good as holding on to the mean.

COMMENTS AND NOTES

Text A has a number of variant characters from B, but they seem to be homophones and/or different ways of writing the same word. Otherwise, Texts A and B are the same.

The Ma-wang-tui texts for line 8 have "Much learning *(to-wen)* means . . ." where the standard text has "Much talk" *(to-yen)*. The contrast is being made, I think, between the mind full of facts and the "empty" space between Heaven and Earth, which is somehow "full" *and* inexhaustible.

The problem of how to read the first four lines is not solved in the Ma-wang-tui texts. One must still choose between a "tough" interpretation, in which Heaven and Earth and the Sage are ruthless in regarding people and things as pawns in a game, versus the "soft" line, where the point is that Heaven and Earth and the Sage see each person and thing as playing a necessary role in the grand cosmic scheme.

Note how the theme of the "seemingly empty continually producing" is continued in chapter 6 (and resumes the opening theme of chapter 4 for that matter).[114]

天地不仁以萬物爲芻狗∠聖人不仁
∠以百省□狗天地□閒□猶囊籥
與虛而不淈蹱而俞出多閒數窮不若
守於中

中

天地不仁以萬物爲芻狗耶人不仁□
百姓爲芻狗天地之閒亓猶囊籥與虛
而不淈勤而俞出多閒數窮不若守於

[CHAPTER 6]

1 The valley[115] spirit never dies;
2 We call it the mysterious female.
3 The gates of the mysterious female—
4 These we call the roots of Heaven and Earth.
5 Subtle yet everlasting! It seems to exist.
6 In being used, it is not exhausted.

COMMENTS AND NOTES

There are no significant differences between Texts A and B, and no significant differences between the Ma-wang-tui version of the chapter and that of the standard text.

[CHAPTER 7]

1 Heaven endures; Earth lasts a long time.
2 The reason why Heaven and Earth can endure and last a long time—
3 Is that they do not live for themselves.
4 Therefore they can long endure.

5 Therefore the Sage:
6 Puts himself in the background yet finds himself in the foreground;
7 Puts self-concern out of [his mind], yet finds self-concern in the fore;
8 Puts self-concern out of [his mind], yet finds that his self-concern is preserved.
9 Is it not because he has no self-interest,
10 That he is therefore able to realize his self-interest?

COMMENTS AND NOTES

Line 7 is not found in Text A and is also not found in any other known edition of the text. It would appear to be copy error.

The opening lines might make more sense if the reader knows that an early Chinese saying about Heaven and Earth was that "Heaven covers and Earth supports," they cover and support the ten thousand things. So they "live" for the sake of other things.

[A]

天長地久天地之所以能□且久者以
其不自生也故能長生乚是以聲人芮
其身而身先乚外其身而身存不以其
无□輿乚故能成其私乚

[B]

天長地久天地之所以能長且久者以
亓不自生也故能長生是以耶人退亓
身而身先外亓身而身先外亓身而身
存不以亓无私輿故能成亓私

[CHAPTER 8]

1 The highest good is like water;
2 Water is good at benefiting the ten thousand things and yet it [does not] compete [with them].
3 It dwells in places the masses of people detest,
4 Therefore it is close to the Way.

5 In dwelling, the good thing is the land;
6 In the mind, the good thing is depth;
7 In giving, the good thing is [being like] Heaven;
8 In speaking, the good thing is sincerity;
9 In governing, the good thing is order;
10 In affairs, the good thing is ability;
11 In activity, the good thing is timeliness.

12 It is only because it does not compete, that therefore it is without fault.

COMMENTS AND NOTES

Both texts omit the negative (*pu*) at the end of line 2: Text A literally has "and yet it has tranquility" (which makes good sense); Text B literally has "and yet it has competition." A number of scholars have argued that the *yu ching* in Text A ("has tranquility") is the intended phrase, and that the *yu* ("has") was changed to *pu* ("does not") only after the *cheng* ("competition") in Text B was understood to be the correct graph.[116] I disagree. For one thing, line 12 assumes that "it does not compete" is a point that was already made, and for another, Text B maintains a clear distinction throughout between *ching* and *cheng*—in all cases where the later, standard text has *ching* (chapters 15, 16, 26, 37, 45, 57, and 61) Text B has *ching*, and in all cases where the later text has *cheng* (chapters 3, 8, 22, 66, 68, 73, and 81) Text B has *cheng*.[117]

In line 3, Text A has simply "masses" instead of "masses of people." Text A contracts lines 7 and 8, giving "In giving the good thing is sincerity." In all other respects, Texts A and B are the same.

The standard text of *Lao-tzu* has *jen* (benevolence, humanity) for *t'ien* (Heaven) at the end of line 7; that is, "In giving the good thing is being humane."

[B]

上善如水〓 善利萬物而有爭居衆人
之所亞故幾於道矣居善地心善淵予
善天言善信正善治事善能動善時夫
唯不爭故无尤

[A]

上善治水〓 善利萬物而有靜居衆之
所惡故幾於道矣∠居善地心善瀟∠
予善信∠正善治∠事善能蹱善時∠
夫唯不靜∠故无尤

[CHAPTER 9]

1 To hold it upright and fill it,
2 Is not so good as stopping [in time].
3 When you pound it out and give it a point,
4 It won't be preserved very long.
5 When gold and jade fill your rooms,
6 You'll never be able to protect them.
7 Arrogance and pride with wealth and rank,
8 On their own bring on disaster.
9 When the deed is accomplished you retire;
10 Such is Heaven's Way!

COMMENTS AND NOTES

Most of lines 2, 3, and 10 are now missing from Text A. Text A omits the "be able" *(neng)* from line 6, giving "You'll never protect them."

There are a number of characters in the Ma-wang-tui versions of this chapter that need to be deciphered (e.g., the first characters in lines 1 and 3—which I translate as "to hold upright" and "pound it out"—and my "point" at the end of line 3). In the present state of research, there seems to be no reason not to see these as meaning roughly the same as their equivalents in later texts.

[B]

植而盈之不若亓已揣而允之不可長
葆也金玉盈室莫之能守也貴富而驕
自遺咎也功述身退天之道也

[A]

□

植而盈之不□□□□□□□□□之□之□
可長葆之乀 金玉盈室莫之守也乀 貴
富而驕自遺咎也乀 功述身芮天□□

[CHAPTER 10]

1 In nourishing the soul[118] and embracing the One—can you do it
without letting them leave?
2 In concentrating your breath and making it soft—can you [make
it like that of] a child?
3 In cultivating and cleaning your profound mirror—can you do it
so that it has no blemish?
4 In loving the people and giving life to the state[119]—can you do
it without using knowledge?
5 In opening and closing the gates of Heaven—can you play the
part of the female?
6 In understanding all within the four reaches—can you do it
without using knowledge?

7 Give birth to them and nourish them.
8 Give birth to them but don't try to own them;
9 Help them to grow but don't rule them.
10 This is called Profound Virtue.

COMMENTS AND NOTES

Very little remains of Text A; all is lost with the exception of the second half of line 2, all of lines 3 and 7, and most of line 8. What remains is exactly the same as what we have in B with the exception
of one variant character.

Since there is no break, no punctuation, between the end of
chapter 9 and the start of chapter 10 in the Ma-wang-tui texts, the
evidence is even clearer, I think, that the *tsai* (or *tai*) at the start of
10 is in fact the last character of 9, and I have put it there as excla-
mation (what it normally means at the end of a line). Thus I think
chapter 10 opens with *ying-p'o pao-i* ("nourishing soul, embracing
the One"); lines 1–6 all have the same form, a four-character phrase
followed by "can you" *(neng)*. The *p'o*, at least in modern belief, is
the "physical soul" (versus the *hun* or spiritual soul), the soul that
stays with or near the body for a while in the grave while the *hun*
goes on through the cycle of rebirth.

In line 3 the Ma-wang-tui texts seem to solve the problem of
whether *lan* means "mirror" or "vision"; the character used in the
Ma-wang-tui texts is understood to mean a bowl of water in which
one can see one's image.

The phrase "without using knowledge" at the end of line 6

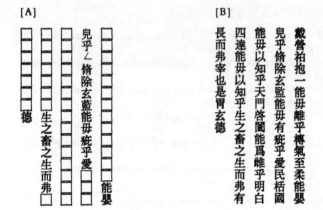

[A]

□□□□□□□德

□□□□□生之畜之生而弗□

□□□□□□脩除玄藍能毋疵乎愛□

兒乎／脩除玄藍能毋疵乎愛□

□□□□□能嬰

[B]

戴營袙抱一能毋離乎専氣至柔能嬰
兒乎脩除玄監能毋有疵乎愛民栝國
能毋以知乎天門啓闔能爲雌乎明白
四達能毋以知乎生之畜之生而弗有
長而弗宰也是胃玄德

where a number of other *Lao-tzu* texts have "without taking action" (*wu-wei*) is a known, in fact common, variant.

The standard *Lao-tzu* text adds a line between lines 8 and 9— "Cause them to act but not be dependent."

[CHAPTER 11]

1 Thirty spokes unite in one hub;
2 It is precisely where there is nothing, that we find the usefulness of the wheel.
3 We fire clay and make vessels;
4 It is precisely where there's no substance, that we find the usefulness of clay pots.
5 We chisel out doors and windows;
6 It is precisely in these empty spaces, that we find the usefulness of the room.
7 Therefore, we regard having something as beneficial;
8 But having nothing as useful.

COMMENTS AND NOTES

Most of lines 1 and 2 are missing in Text A along with all of line 5.

It has long been thought that the variant single character "thirty" in line 1 (*sa*) in place of the normal two-character phrase *san-shih* ("three tens") resulted from later attempts to pare down the number of characters in the text as a whole. But *sa* is what we find in the Ma-wang-tui texts.

In line 3 where the standard text has "to mix clay" (*yen*) the Ma-wang-tui texts have a character that seems to mean "bake" or "fire" (*jan*).

Line 5 in the standard text of *Lao-tzu* reads, "We bore out doors and windows *to make a room*." The parallelism with the other lines seems to demand these words, but they are not found in the Ma-wang-tui texts.

卅楅同一轂當亓无有車之用也埏埴
而爲器當亓无有埴器之用也鑿户牖
當亓无有室之用也故有之爲利无之
以爲用∠

卅□□□□其无□之用□然埴
爲器當其无有埴器□□□□□當
其无有□之用也故有之以爲利无之
以爲用

[CHAPTER 12]

1 The five colors cause one's eyes to go blind.
2 Racing horses and hunting cause one's mind to go mad.
3 Goods that are hard to obtain pose an obstacle to one's travels.
4 The five flavors confuse one's palate.
5 The five tones cause one's ears to go **deaf.**

6 Therefore, in the government of the Sage:
7 He's for the belly and not for the eyes.
8 Thus he rejects that and takes this.

COMMENTS AND NOTES

Text A has "see clearly" (*ming*) for "blind" (*mang*) in line 1 in what must be copyist error.

The order of lines 1–5 differs in the Ma-wang-tui texts from what we normally find. In the standard *Lao-tzu* the sequence is 1, 5, 4, 2, 3. One might surmise that a later editor went to that sequence to put the three "five" lines together. The five colors are green, red, yellow, white, and black: the five flavors are sweet, bitter, salty, sour, and pungent: the five tones are the tones of the Chinese musical scale, C, D, E, G, and A.

Line 6 in the standard *Lao-tzu* simply says, "Therefore the Sage," not "Therefore *in the government of* the Sage." This is one of several places in the Ma-wang-tui texts where they seem more directly concerned with governing than do later editions of the *Lao-tzu*.

五色使人目盲馳騁田臘使人心發狂
難得之貨○使人之行仿五味使人之
口爽五音使人之耳□是以即人之治
也爲腹而不爲目故去彼而取此

五色使人目明∠馳騁田臘使人□□
□難得之貨使人之行方五味使人之
口啊∠五音使人之耳聾∠是以聲人
之治也爲腹不□□故去罷耳此

[CHAPTER 13]

1 "Regard favor and disgrace with alarm."
2 "Respect great distress as you do your own person."
3 What do I mean when I say "Regard favor and disgrace with alarm"?
4 Favor is inferior.
5 If you get it—be alarmed!
6 If you lose it—be alarmed!
7 This is what I mean when I say "Regard favor and disgrace with alarm."
8 What do I mean when I say "Respect great distress as you do your own person"?
9 The reason why I have great distress
10 Is that I have a body.
11 If I had no body, what distress would I have?
12 Therefore, to one who values acting for himself over acting on behalf of the world,
13 You can entrust the world.
14 And to one who in being parsimonious regards his person as equal to the world,
15 You can turn over the world.

COMMENTS AND NOTES

Text A has a number of different graphs in various places, but the intended word and meaning would seem to be the same in each case.

In a few editions of the *Lao-tzu* line 4 reads, "Favor is superior; disgrace is inferior." That reading is not confirmed by these texts. Line 4, nonetheless, feels out of place—like an editorial aside.

The wording of line 12 differs markedly from what we find in other editions. Normally, lines 12 and 14 are strictly parallel. For example, Wing-tsit Chan's translation reads this way: "Therefore he who values the world as his body may be entrusted with the empire. He who loves the world as his body may be entrusted with the empire."[120] Although there are a number of different arrangements of the wording in lines 12–15 in other texts, the Ma-wang-tui version of line 12 is unique.

The sentiments of chapter 13—that the person who should be entrusted with ruling the world is precisely the one who cares more for his own life than he does for the wealth, honor, and power he

龍辱若驚貴大梡若身　苛胃龍辱若
驚龍之爲下得之若驚失□若驚∠是
胃龍辱若驚何胃貴大梡若身吾所以
有大梡者爲吾有身也及吾无身有何
梡故貴爲身於爲天下∠若可以迵天
下矣∠愛以身爲天下女可以寄天下

弄辱若驚貴大患若身何胃弄辱若驚
弄之爲下也得之若驚失之若驚是胃
弄辱若驚何胃貴大患若身吾所以有
大患者爲吾有身也及吾無身有何患
故貴爲身於爲天下若可以橐天下□
愛以身爲天下女可以寄天下矣

would have by ruling the world—show up again in the *Chuang-tzu* in a section that A. C. Graham identifies as "Yangist" (representing the views of the "individualist" Yang Chu). The first anecdote in chapter 28 of the *Chuang-tzu* reads, "Yao resigned the empire to Hsü Yu. Hsü Yu refused it. Next he resigned it to Tzu-chou Chih-fu. 'It might not be a bad idea to make me Son of Heaven,' said Tzu-chou Chih-fu. 'However, at the moment I am worried about a serious ailment. I'm going to put it right, and haven't time just now to put the empire right.' The empire is the most important thing of all, but he would not harm his life for the sake of it, and how much less for anything else! Only the man who cares nothing for the empire deserves to be entrusted with the empire."[121]

[CHAPTER 14]

1 We look at it but do not see it;
2 We **name** this "the minute."
3 We listen to it but do not hear it;
4 We name this "the rarefied."
5 We touch it but do not hold it;
6 We name this "the level and smooth."

7 These three cannot be examined to the limit.
8 Thus they merge together as one.
9 "One"—there is nothing more encompassing above it,
10 And nothing smaller below it.
11 Boundless, formless! It cannot be named,
12 And returns to the state of no-thing.

13 This is called the formless form,
14 The substanceless image.
15 This is called the subtle and indistinct.
16 Follow it and you won't see its back;
17 Greet it and you won't see its head.
18 Hold on to the Way of the present—
19 To manage the things of the present,
20 And to know the ancient beginning.
21 This is called the beginning of the thread of the Way.

COMMENTS AND NOTES

Parts of lines 8, 14, 15, 16, and 21 are missing in Text A; there are also a couple of variant characters that distinguish A from B, but those words appear to mean the same thing in both texts.

There are a number of ways in which the Ma-wang-tui version of chapter 14 differs from what we find in the standard text. To begin with, the qualities "level and smooth" and "minute" are reversed in lines 2 and 6, and the word "this" or "these" *(tz'u)* is not found at the head of line 7 in the Ma-wang-tui texts (even though one must put it there in translation).

More importantly, at the start of line 9, the "One" *(i-che)* is singled out for attention (the words *i-che* are omitted in later editions), and lines 9 and 10 in the Ma-wang-tui texts seem to say, "There is nothing more encompassing above it, and nothing more minute be-

[A]

是胃□□□

□□□□□□□□□□而不見其

首執今之道以御今之有乀以知古始

歸於无物乀是胃无狀之狀无物之□

做乀其下不物乀尋﹦呵不可名也復

者不可至計乀故圓□□﹦者其上不

名之曰希撋之而弗得名之曰夷乀三

視之而弗見名之曰䍐聽之而弗聞乀

[B]

道以御今之有以知古始是胃道紀

隨而不見示後迎而不見示首執今之

物是胃无狀之狀无物之象是胃沕望

示下不物尋﹦呵不可命也復歸於无

不可至計故緄而爲一﹦者示上不謬

之曰希○撋之而弗得命之曰夷三者

視之而弗見□之曰微聽之而弗聞命

---

low it"—which is true, of course, of the number one—versus the normal "Its top is not dazzling; its bottom is not dark."[122]

Lines 16 and 17 are normally reversed, and the standard *Lao-tzu* text has "Hold on to the Way of the *past*" in line 18, not the Way of the *present*. Finally, the grammatical particles used in lines 19 and 20 make it clear that these are two parallel things—that is to say, by holding on to the Way of the present one can (a) manage the things of the present and (b) know the ancient beginning. The particles used in the standard text allow for a different interpretation—"Hold fast to the way of antiquity, In order to keep in control the realm of today. The ability to know the beginning of antiquity, Is called the thread running through the way."[123]

CHAPTER 15

1 The one who was skilled at practicing the Way in antiquity,
2 Was subtle and profound, mysterious and penetratingly wise.
3 His depth cannot be known.
4 It is only because he cannot be known
5 That therefore were I forced to describe him I'd say:

6 Hesitant was he! Like someone crossing a river in winter.
7 Undecided was he! As though in fear of his neighbors on all four sides.
8 Solemn and polite was he! Like a guest.
9 Scattered and dispersed was he! Like ice as it melts.
10 Genuine, unformed was he! Like uncarved wood.
11 Merged, undifferentiated was he! Like muddy water.
12 Broad and expansive was he! Like a valley.

13 If you take muddy water and still it, it gradually becomes clear.
14 If you bring something to rest in order to move it, it gradually comes alive.
15 *The one who* preserves this Way **does not** desire to be full;
16 Therefore he can wear out with no need to be renewed.

COMMENTS AND NOTES

A number of character variants distinguish Texts A and B, but they seem unimportant. But Text A had an additional phrase between lines 15 and 16, which apparently said, "Now it is only because he does not desire [to be full, that] therefore . . ." *(fu wei pu-yü* □ □ *i).*

Most texts of the *Lao-tzu* have "The one who was skilled at being a ruler [or 'knight/scribe'—*shih*] in antiquity" in line 1: The variant phrase of *wei-tao* ("practicing the Way") for *wei-shih* ("being a ruler") is known but uncommon. The same holds true for the sequence of lines 11 and 12: they are normally reversed. The sequence of 12 and 11 nicely juxtaposes the "muddy water" of lines 11 and 13.

Almost all texts of the *Lao-tzu* have *shu-neng* ("Who can," "Who is able to . . .") at the head of lines 13 and 14. Thus Wing-tsit Chan's translation reads, "Who can make muddy water gradually clear through tranquility? Who can make the still gradually come to life through activity?"[124] Those words are not found in the Ma-

[B]

成

徐生葆此道□□欲盈是以能獘而不

湛呵亓若浴濁而靜之徐清女以重之

呵亓若淩澤沌呵亓若樸湷呵亓若濁

涉水猷呵亓若畏四琝嚴呵亓若客涣

唯不可志故强爲之容曰與呵亓若冬

古之仚爲道者微眇玄達深不可志夫

[A]

欲□□以能□□成

女以重之余生葆此道不欲盈夫唯不

□□□□若浴ㄥ濁而情之余清ㄥ

ㄥ涣呵其若淩澤□

冬□□□□□畏四□□呵其若客

唯不可志故强爲之容ㄥ曰與呵其若

□□□□□□□□□深不可志夫

wang-tui texts. And later texts of the *Lao-tzu* agree with Text A in adding the phrase "It is only because he does not desire to be full" between lines 15 and 16.

[CHAPTER 16]

1 Take emptiness to the limit;
2 Maintain tranquility in the center.[125]

3 The ten thousand things—side-by-side they arise;
4 And by this I see their return.
5 Things [come forth] in great numbers;
6 Each one returns to its root.
7 This is called tranquility.
8 "Tranquility"—This means to return to your fate.
9 To return to your fate is to be constant;
10 To know the constant is to be wise.
11 Not to know the constant is to be reckless and wild;
12 If you're reckless and wild, your actions will lead to misfortune.

13 To know the constant is to be all-embracing;
14 To be all-embracing is to be impartial;
15 To be impartial is to be kingly;
16 **To be kingly is to be** [like] Heaven;
17 To be [like] Heaven is to be [one with] the Tao;
18 If you're [one with] the Tao, to the end of your days you'll suffer
    no harm.

COMMENTS AND NOTES

Lines 1 and 2 in the Ma-wang-tui texts seem to read as definitions.
They are grammatically parallel to lines 9 and 10 and might be translated, "To reach emptiness is what we mean by the extreme; To
maintain tranquility is what we mean by the center." But the first
part of this chapter makes more sense if lines 1 and 2 are rather understood as admonitions to someone practicing meditation (see the
Introduction on this point).

Text A has "surface" *(piao)* in line 2 where Text B reads "center" *(tu*—literally "oversee"), but it is likely that in both cases the
same word is intended (for more on this point see note 125).

At the start of line 5 both texts literally say, "Heaven's things"
(or "the things of nature"—*t'ien-wu*), but *t'ien* is probably a mistake
for the standard word *fu* ("The" or "Now the . . .").

In line 7 we normally find the words "To return to its root"
(kuei-ken) repeated before the words "This is called tranquility"
(yüeh-ching); but here they are not. By way of contrast, the word

[A]

至虛極也守情表也萬物旁作吾以觀

其復也天物雲＝ 各復歸於其□□

＝是胃復＝ 命＝ 常也知常明也不知

常帚＝ 作兇知常容＝ 乃公＝ 乃王＝

乃天＝ 乃道□ □□沕身不怠

[B]

至虛極也守靜督也萬物旁作吾以觀

亓復也天物祘＝ 各復歸於亓根曰靜

＝是胃復＝ 命＝ 常也知常明也不知

常芒＝ 作凶知常容＝ 乃公＝ 乃王□

天＝ 乃道＝ 乃沒身不殆

---

wang ("wild and reckless") is repeated in the Ma-wang-tui texts, giving us two lines (11 and 12) where we normally have only one (e.g., Wing-tsit Chan translates, "Not to know the eternal is to act blindly to result in disaster."[126])

Finally, at the end of the chapter later *Lao-tzu* texts have one more "to be this is to be this"—namely, "To be [one with] the Tao is to be long lasting" *(tao nai chiu)*, and then they say, "and to the end of your days . . ."

Note that the word *kung* ("impartial") in line 14—chosen to rhyme with the "all-embracing" *(jung)* of the previous line—also means "duke." This allows the author to shift emphasis and move up through a hierarchy of powers—from duke to king to Heaven to the Tao.

[CHAPTER 17]

Chapters 17, 18, and 19 should be read together as a unit.

1 With the highest [kind of rulers], those below simply know **they** exist.
2 With those **one step down**—they love and praise them.
3 With those one further step down—they fear them.
4 And with those at the bottom—they ridicule and insult them.

5 When trust is insufficient, there will be no trust [in return].
6 Hesitant, undecided! Like this is his respect for speaking.
7 He completes his tasks and finishes his affairs,[127]
8 Yet the common people say, "These things all happened by nature."

COMMENTS AND NOTES

In line 4 the Ma-wang-tui texts have "those at the bottom" *(ch'i-hsia)* where the standard text has one final "next down" *(ch'i tz'u)*. In line 5 the standard text ends with "in him" *(yen)*, but the Ma-wang-tui texts omit that word. Finally, in line 8, many *Lao-tzu* texts say "the common people *all* say"; but the omission of "all," as we find here, is a known form of the line.

大上下知又□亓□親譽之亓次畏之
亓下母之信不足安有不信猷呵亓貴
言也成功遂事而百姓胃我自然

大上下知有之其次親譽之其次畏之
其下母之信不足案有不信□□其貴
言也成功遂事而百省胃我自然∠

CHAPTER 18

Chapters 17, 18, and 19 should be read together as a unit.

1 Therefore, when the Great Way is rejected, it is then that we
   have the virtues of humanity and righteousness;
2 When knowledge and wisdom appear, it is then that there is
   great hypocrisy;
3 When the six relations are not in harmony, it is then that we have
   filial piety and compassion;
4 And when the country is in chaos and confusion, it is then that
   there are virtuous officials.

COMMENTS AND NOTES

At the end of line 3, Text A has *hsü* ("nurture") where Text B has
hsiao ("filial piety"), giving "then we have nurture and compassion
[or nurturing compassion]." (The "six relations" [*liu-ch'in*] are father,
son, older brother, younger brother, husband, and wife.) In line 4,
"country" is *kuo-chia* in Text B; *pang-chia* in Text A. Text B consis-
tently writes *kuo* for *pang* to avoid the taboo on the personal name of
Han Kao-tsu (r. 206–194 B.C.), Liu Pang.

The "Therefore" *(ku)* in line 1 does not occur in other editions
of the *Lao-tzu*: it is a clear indication that chapter 18 follows directly
from the things said in chapter 17. Also, the Ma-wang-tui texts have
an *an* ("then") in the middle of every line to emphasize that "it is
only then that such bad things happen"; that *an* does not occur in the
standard text of *Lao-tzu*.

Finally, the variant of "virtuous officials" *(chen-ch'en)* for "loyal
officials" *(chung-ch'en)* is a known but uncommon substitution.

The translator must make a number of choices in translating
this chapter that unfortunately suggest different interpretations of
Taoist philosophical views. For one thing, one must choose between
putting the entire message in past or present tense. I have opted for
the present, but one could equally say, "When the Great Tao *was* rejected," and so on, and it is true that Taoists do assume that back at
the beginning of time all things were in accord with the Way and that
the establishment of principles of conduct coincided with the decline
of the Way. But the Taoists also assume that the Way can still be followed and that in some way the Way is something that is rejected or
forgotten by individuals in their individual lives as they mature.

[B]

臣

六親不和安又孝茲國家閻亂安有貞

故大道廢安有仁義知慧出安有□□

[A]

案有貞臣

大偽六親不和案有畜茲邦家閻乱∠

故大道廢∠案有仁義知快出∠案有

It is unclear in most Taoist writings if, in antiquity, the Great Way was actively *rejected* or just *declined* (by nature; that is, on its own). The verb used here, *fei*, and the grammatical form—*ta-tao fei*—suggest the former.

Chapters 17, 18, and 19 should be read together as a unit.

1 Eliminate sageliness, throw away knowledge,
2 And the people will benefit a hundredfold.
3 Eliminate humanity, throw away righteousness,
4 And the people will return to filial piety and compassion.
5 Eliminate craftiness, throw away profit,
6 Then we will have no robbers and thieves.

7 These three sayings—
8 Regarded as a text are not yet complete.
9 Thus, we must see to it that they have the following appended:

10 Manifest plainness and embrace the genuine;
11 Lessen *self-interest* and make few your desires;
12 Eliminate learning and have no undue concern.

COMMENTS AND NOTES

Text A is like the standard text in omitting the *erh*'s ("And") at the head of lines 2 and 4. In line 4, Text A again has "nurture" *(hsü)* where Text B has "compassion."

The Ma-wang-tui texts have "These three *sayings*" *(san-yen)* in line 7 where the standard text has simply "These three" *(san-che)*, and in line 8, they have "not yet complete" *(wei-tsu)* where the standard text has simply "not complete" *(pu-tsu)*.

Commentators and translators have gone back and forth on the issue of whether or not the first line of chapter 20 ("Eliminate learning and have no concern") is in fact the last line of chapter 19. I think it is. The lack of punctuation in the Ma-wang-tui texts adds support for this cause. Moreover, it has always been clear that this line rhymes with lines 10 and 11 in chapter 19 (the rhyme words are *p'u* ["genuine"], *yü* ["desires"], and *yu* ["anxiety"]). Finally, if the "text" has "three sayings," then there should be *three* appended lines as well.

[B]

絶耶棄知而民利百倍絶仁棄義而民
復孝茲絶巧棄利盜賊无有此三言也
以爲文未足故令之有所屬見素抱樸
少□而寡欲

[A]

絶聲棄知民利百負∠絶仁棄義民復
畜茲∠絶巧棄利盜賊无有此三言也
以爲文未足∠故令之有所屬見素抱

□
□
□
□
□

[232]

[CHAPTER 20]

1 Agreement and angry rejection;
2 How great is the difference between them?
3 Beautiful and ugly;
4 What's it like—the difference between them?
5 The one who is feared by others,
6 Must also because of this fear other men.
7 Wild, unrestrained! It will never come to an end!

8 The multitudes are peaceful and happy;
9 Like climbing a terrace in springtime to feast at the t'ai-lao sacrifice.
10 But I'm tranquil and quiet—not yet having given any sign.
11 Like a child who has not yet smiled.
12 Tired and exhausted—as though I have no place to return.
13 The multitudes all have a surplus.
[13a **I alone seem to be lacking**.]
14 Mine is the mind of a fool—ignorant and stupid!
15 The common people see things clearly;
16 I alone am in the dark.
17 The common people discriminate and make fine distinctions;
18 I alone am muddled and confused.
19 Formless am I! Like the ocean;
20 Shapeless am I! As though I have nothing in which I can rest.
21 The masses all have their reasons [for acting];
22 I alone am stupid and obstinate like a rustic.
23 But my desires <u>alone</u> differ from those of others—
24 For I value drawing sustenance from the Mother.

COMMENTS AND NOTES

Much of Text A is now missing. Missing through deterioration are parts of lines 5 and 6, all of lines 7 and 11, parts of lines 12, 13, 15, 16, and 22, and all of line 21. Text A is like the standard text in having a line between lines 13 and 14—"I alone seem to be lacking" *(wo tu i)*: the omission of this line in Text B is surely an error.

On moving the first line of chapter 20 in the standard text of *Lao-tzu* to the end of chapter 19, see the notes to chapter 19.

[A]

□□□唯與訶其相去幾何美與惡
其相去何若人之□□亦不□□
□□衆人巸=若鄉於大牢
乚而春登臺我泊焉未垗若
累呵如□□皆有餘我獨遺我
愚人之心也惷=呵□□
□呵鬻人蔡= 我獨閩= 呵物呵其若
䐗呵鬻人蔡= 我獨閩= 呵物呵其若
墾呵其若无所止□□
□以悝吾欲獨異於人而貴食母

[B]

絕學无憂唯呵亓相去幾何美與亞
亓相去何若人之所畏亦不可以不畏
人朢呵亓未央才衆人巸= 若鄉於大
牢而春登臺我博焉未垗若嬰兒未咳
纍呵佁无所歸衆人皆有余我愚人之
心也湷= 呵鬻人昭= 我獨若闒呵鬻
人蔡= 我獨閩= 呵淴呵亓若海朢呵
若无所止衆人皆有以我獨門元以鄙
吾欲獨異於人而貴食母

Significantly, the Ma-wang-tui texts have "beautiful and ugly"
(*mei yü o*) in line 3 where the standard text has "good and bad" (*shan
yü o*) (though "beautiful and ugly" is an attested reading). Moreover,
in line 1, Text A has *ho* ("angry rejection") in place of *a* ("no"), giving the present reading (the graph in Text B is understood to mean
the same). And the addition of the words that mean "also" and
"other men" at the beginning and end of line 6 give the reading of
"The one who is feared by others, Must also because of this fear
other men" versus the seemingly irrelevant line "The things people
fear cannot not be feared."

In lines 19 and 20, the Ma-wang-tui texts have *hu* ("formless")

[234]

and *huang* [actually *wang*] ("shapeless") where other texts normally have *tan* ("quiet and tranquil") and *liu* ("a high wind"). And in line 23 the change from *wo* ("I") at the start of the line to *wu-yū* ("my desires") gives us the present reading versus the normal "I alone differ from others."

[CHAPTER 21]

1 The character of great virtue follows alone from the Way.
2 As for the nature of the Way—it's shapeless and formless.
3 Formless! Shapeless! Inside there are images.
4 Shapeless! Formless! Inside there are things.
5 Hidden! Obscure! Inside there are essences.
6 These essences are very real;
7 Inside them is the proof.

8 From the present back to the past,
9 Its name has never gone away.
10 It is by this that we comply with the father of the multitude [of things].
11 How do I know that the father of the multitude is so?
12 By this.

COMMENTS AND NOTES

Text A is essentially the same as Text B. There are a number of character variants in both texts that at this stage of our research seem best identified with the characters we find in the standard text.

Both Ma-wang-tui texts literally say, "The things of the Way" (*tao chih wu*) at the start of line 2 where later editions have "As for the nature of the Way [literally—As for the Way's being a thing]" (*tao chih wei wu*). My feeling is that the *wei* was mistakenly left out in both Ma-wang-tui texts, since the basic unit throughout the chapter is the four-character line.

The standard text of *Lao-tzu* has "From the past to the present" in line 8; it now seems clear that the reverse form is correct since the last words in lines 8, 9, and 10 all would have rhymed ("past"/*ku*, "gone away"/*ch'ü*, "father"/*fu*).

For line 10 the standard text has "It is this we use to examine the origins of the multitude."

[B]

孔德之容唯道是從道之物唯望沕
＝呵望呵中又象呵望呵沕呵中有物
呵幼呵冥呵元中有請呵元請甚真元
中有信自今及古元名不去以順衆父
吾何以知衆父之然也以此

[A]

孔德之容唯道是從道之物唯望唯物
□□□呵中有象呵望呵物呵中有物
呵∠滰呵鳴呵中有請吔∠其請甚真
其中□□自今及古其名不去以順衆
仅∠吾何以知衆仅之然以此∠

[CHAPTER 24]

1 One who boasts is not established;
2 One who shows himself off does not become prominent;
3 One who puts himself on display does not brightly shine;
4 One who brags about himself gets no credit;
5 One who praises himself does not long endure.

6 In the Way, such things are called:
7 "Surplus food and redundant action."
8 And with things—there are those who hate them.
9 Therefore, the one with the Way in them does not dwell.

COMMENTS AND NOTES

Text A omits the character "the one who" (*che*) in line 2; otherwise the two texts appear to have been identical.

The Ma-wang-tui texts have "to cook" (*ch'ui*) in line 1 where other texts have "to stand on tiptoe" (*ch'i*). The intended character is surely the *ch'ui* that means "to blow" but also "to boast or to brag": The entire chapter, after all, concerns egotism. Chou Tz'u-chi[128] and Hsü K'ang-sheng[129] both read *ch'ui* as a mistake for *ch'i*. D. C. Lau[130] has "He who blows cannot stand." It is interesting that the Chinese word for "blow" could come to mean "boast or brag" and that one of our own words for a braggart is a "blowhard."

Line 2 in the standard text is "He who strides forward does not go";[131] that line does not occur in the Ma-wang-tui texts. Moreover, the order of lines 1–5 is not the same as what we normally find. The usual order is 1, extra line, 3, 2, 4, 5. The "shows himself off" (*shih*) in line 2 in the Ma-wang-tui texts in other texts of the *Lao-tzu* is rather "sees himself as right" (*shih*).

In line 9, the Ma-wang-tui texts literally say, "Therefore, *the one who has desires* . . ." (*yu-yü-che*), where all other texts say, "The one who has the Tao." Arguments by others to the contrary, I persist in thinking that "desires" here is a mistake for the "Way," perhaps the result of the fact that the small seal forms of "desires" and "Way" are not all that dissimilar. Note that lines 8 and 9 occur again, verbatim, at the start of chapter 31, and again the Ma-wang-tui texts say, "the one who has desires."

D. C. Lau makes sense of the phrase by translating "a man of ambition."[132] Hsü K'ang-sheng[133] shares my opinion that "the one with desires" is not consistent with the thought of the text. Chou

[B]

炊者不立自視者不章自見者不明自
伐者无功自矜者不長示在道也曰粽
食贅行物或亞之故有欲者弗居

[A]

炊者不立自視不章□見者不明∠自
伐者无功自矜者不長其在道曰粽食
贅行∠物或惡之故有欲者□居∠

Tz'u-chi, on the other hand, if I understand him correctly, would translate the last line "Therefore those with desires do not dwell *in it*,"[134] with the "it" meaning the Tao—still meaning that "having desires" is not a good thing.

[CHAPTER 22]

1   Bent over, you'll be preserved whole;
2   When twisted, you'll be upright;
3   When hollowed out, you'll be full;
4   When worn out, you'll be renewed;
5   When you have little, you'll attain [much];
6   With much, you'll be confused.

7   Therefore the Sage holds on to the One and in this way becomes the shepherd of the world.
8   He does not show himself off; therefore he becomes prominent.
9   He does not put himself on display; therefore he brightly shines.
10   He does not brag about himself; therefore he receives credit.
11   He does not praise his own deeds; therefore he can long endure.

12   It is only because he does not compete that, therefore, no one is able to compete with him.
13   The so-called "Bent over you'll be preserved whole" of the ancients
14   Was an expression that was really close to it!
15   Truly "wholeness" will belong to him.

COMMENTS AND NOTES

Text A, in what must be a copy error, has "Bent over then *gold*" (or "metal"—*chin*) in line 1 instead of "whole" *(ch'üan)*, and in line 2, Text A has "settled/still" *(ting)* instead of "upright" *(cheng)*. In lines 8 and 9, Text A reverses the qualities of "prominent" *(chang)* and "brightly shine" *(ming)*, in this way according with later editions. Most of line 13 is now missing from Text A.

Most editions of the *Lao-tzu* have "direct" or "straight" *(chih)* in line 2 where Text A has "still" *(ting)* and Text B "upright" *(cheng)*, and lines 8 and 9 are normally reversed, with the standard text here (as in chapter 24 above) again having "does not see himself as right" *(pu tzu-shih)* in the present line 8 instead of "does not put himself on display" (also *pu tzu-shih).*

In what may be an important variant, the Ma-wang-tui texts have "hold on to the One" *(chih-i)* in line 7 where all other known texts have "embrace the One" *(pao-i).* It has been argued that "hold on to the One" is a Legalist phrase, but the evidence is not conclusive.[135] Also in line 7, the Ma-wang-tui texts tell us the Sage will in

曲則全汪則正洼則盈斃則新少則得
多則惑是以耶人執一以爲天下牧不
自視故章不自見也故明不自伐故有
功弗矜故能長夫唯不爭故莫能與之
爭古之所胃曲全者幾語才誠全歸之

曲則金乚枉則定乚洼則盈敝則新乚
少則得乚多則惑乚是以聲人執一以
爲天下牧不□視故明不自見故章不
自伐故有功乚弗矜故能長乚夫唯不
爭故莫能與之爭古□□□□□□
語才乚誠金歸之

---

this way become the "shepherd" (mu) of the world, not its "model" (shih); with "shepherd" being a known reference to the ruler in the political writings of the time, the sayings in this chapter would seem to have a specific, political focus instead of a general one. (On the "shepherding" of the ruler note also the comments above, on chapter 61.)

The Ma-wang-tui texts have "he does not praise them" (fu-chin) at the start of line 11 where later editions say "he does not praise himself" (pu tzu-chin).

The words "the world" (t'ien-hsia) are normally found in line 12—namely, "that, therefore, no one in the world is able to compete with him"; they do not occur here.

Finally, lines 14 and 15 are somewhat different in the Ma-wang-tui texts from what we normally find. Line 14 normally reads, "How can these be false words?!" (*ch'i hsü-yen tsai*). The rhetorical particle *ch'i* does not occur in the Ma-wang-tui texts (though it might be implied) and for "false" they read rather *chi*—which means either "close to/almost" or "auspicious" (the suggestions, respectively, of Hsü K'ang-sheng[136] and Chou Tz'u-chi[137]). Also, in line 15 the omission of the particle *erh* ("and") seems to make the last line one clause instead of two (Chan translates, "Truly he will be preserved and [prominence and credit] will come to him."[138])

One way in which the paradox "Bent over, you'll be preserved whole" is seen to be true is illustrated by the story of "Crippled Shu" in chapter 4 of the *Chuang-tzu*. In Watson's translation that reads, "There's Crippled Shu—chin stuck down in his navel, shoulders up above his head, pigtail pointing at the sky, his five organs on the top, his two thighs pressing his ribs. By sewing and washing, he gets enough to fill his mouth; by handling a winnow and sifting out the good grain, he makes enough to feed ten people. When the authorities call out the troops, he stands in the crowd waving good-bye; when they get up a big work party, they pass him over because he's a chronic invalid. And when they are doling out grain to the ailing, he gets three big measures and ten bundles of firewood. With a crippled body, he's still able to look after himself and finish out the years Heaven gave him. How much better, then, if he had crippled virtue!"[139]

CHAPTER 23

1 To rarely speak—such is [the way of] Nature.
2 Fierce winds don't last the whole morning;
3 Torrential rains don't last the whole day.
4 Who makes these things?
5 If even Heaven and Earth can't make these last long—
6 How much the more is this true for man?!

7 Therefore, one who devotes himself to the Way is one with the
   Way;
8 One who [devotes himself to] Virtue is one with that Virtue;
9 And one who [devotes himself to] losing is one with that loss.
10 To the one who is one with Virtue, the Way also gives Virtue;
11 While for the one who is one with his loss, the Way also
   disregards him.

COMMENTS AND NOTES

The author clearly plays with the double meaning of *te* ("virtue" but
also "gain" or "attain") in lines 8 and 10. The word *te* allows the author to move back and forth between the pairs of "the Way and
Virtue" on the one hand and "gain and loss" on the other. Thus,
lines 8–10 also mean:

8 One who [devotes himself to] attaining is one with that gain;
9 And one who [devotes himself to] losing is one with that loss.
10 With the one who is one with his attainment, the Way also gets
   him.
11 While for the one who is one with his loss, the Way also
   disregards him.

The "devotes himself to" *(ts'ung-shih)* is as one would do with a
career. "Virtue" in this context is probably best understood as the
"power" of the Way in things, not moral virtue. Thus some people
might be more intent on using the power of the Way in themselves than
in being one with the Way. In this sense, line 10 might best be read as
"To the one who is one with Virtue, the Way also empowers him."
   Line 9 in Text A mistakenly begins, "The one who, the one
who" *(che che)* instead of "The one who [devotes himself to] losing"
(shih-che). In all other respects, what survives of Text A does not differ from Text B in any significant way.

[A]

希言自然飄風不冬朝暴雨不冬日之
執爲此天地□□□□□於□□故
從事而道者同於道德者同於德者
同於失∠同於德□道亦德之同於失
者道亦失之

[B]

希言自然飄風不冬朝暴雨不冬日執
爲此天地而弗能久有兄於人乎故從
事而道者同於道德者同於德失者同
於失同於德者道亦德之同於失者道
亦失之

There is a "Therefore" at the start of line 2 in the standard text; however, the omission of that word is common.

In line 4 in the standard text the author answers his question—"Heaven and Earth"—the characters "Heaven and Earth" then being repeated at the start of line 5. But the question is really rhetorical and the reader already knows the answer.

While lines 7, 8, and 9 in the standard text are essentially the same as we have here, after line 9 that text is quite different grammatically and in terms of content. Wing-tsit Chan's translation serves well to point up the differences:

He who is identified with Tao—Tao is also happy to have him.
He who is identified with virtue—virtue is also happy to have him.
And he who is identified with the abandonment (of Tao)—the
    abandonment (of Tao) is also happy to abandon him.[140]

There is nothing in the Ma-wang-tui texts that corresponds with the first line, and there is no mention of anything being "happy." Moreover, in lines 10 and 11 in the Ma-wang-tui texts it is the Way that does something in the second part of each line, not Virtue (or attainment) and abandonment.

Finally, note that the final line in the chapter in later editions of the text—"It is only when one does not have enough faith in others that others will have no faith in him"[141]—does not occur in the Ma-wang-tui texts.

CHAPTER 25

1 There was something formed out of chaos,
2 That was born before Heaven and Earth.
3 Quiet and still! Pure and deep!
4 It stands on its own and doesn't change.
5 It can be regarded as the mother of Heaven and Earth.
6 I do not yet know its name:
7 I "style" it "the Way."
8 Were I forced to give it a name, I would call it "the Great."

9 "Great" means "to depart";
10 "To depart" means "to be far away";
11 And "to be far away" means "to return."

12 The Way is great;
13 Heaven is great;
14 Earth is great;
15 And the king is also great.
16 In the country there are four greats, and the king occupies one place among them.

17 Man models himself on the Earth;
18 The Earth models itself on Heaven;
19 Heaven models itself on the Way;
20 And the Way models itself on that which is so on its own.

COMMENTS AND NOTES

Text A appears to have been exactly the same as Text B, but portions of lines 3, 11, 12, and 18–20 are now missing.

The standard text adds a line between lines 4 and 5—"It operates everywhere and is free from danger."[142] Also, in line 5, almost all other editions of the *Lao-tzu* have "the mother of the world" *(t'ien-hsia)* instead of "the mother of Heaven and Earth."

In line 6 the Ma-wang-tui texts have the negative *wei* ("not yet" or "never") where other texts have the simple *pu* ("do not"), giving the reading "I do not yet know [or I have never known] its name," instead of "I do not know its name," the distinction drawn in lines 6–8 between that of "name" *(ming)* and "style" *(tzu)* being the distinction made in ancient China between a man's name and his style. The "name" is given at birth, is very formal and rarely used in public address; the "style" is taken at "capping" age, when a young man

法□法□

四大而王居一焉∠人法地□法□

□□□天大地大王亦大國中有

曰道吾強爲之名曰大□曰筮□曰□

□可以爲天地母吾未知其名字之

有物昆成先天地生繡呵繆呵獨立□

法道□法自然

有四大而王居一焉人法地□法天□

遠□曰反道大天大地大王亦大國中

之曰道吾強爲之名曰大□曰筮□曰

不玹可以爲天地母吾未知亓名字

有物昆成先天地生蕭呵漻呵獨立而

becomes an adult, and is commonly used in public address with friends who are on familiar terms.

The standard text has a "Therefore" at the start of line 12, and in line 16 has "in the realm" (*yü-chung*) where the Ma-wang-tui texts have "in the country" (or "state"—*kuo-chung*).

Readers of this chapter are sometimes troubled by the fact that the last line seems to present us with something that is even superior to the Way—"that which is so on its own" (*tzu-jan*—sometimes translated as "nature"). I think this is just another way of saying that the Way is that reality that truly *exists* out of its own power, the one and only thing that does not depend for its existence on other things.

[CHAPTER 26]

1 The heavy is the root of the light;
2 Tranquility is the lord of agitation.

3 Therefore the gentleman, in traveling all day, does not get far away from his luggage carts.
4 When he's safely inside a walled-in [protected] hostel and resting at ease—only then does he transcend all concern.
5 How can the king of ten thousand chariots treat his own person more lightly than the whole land?!

6 If you regard things too lightly, then you lose the basic;
7 If you're agitated, you lose the "lord."

COMMENTS AND NOTES

The last line not only refers back to the point made in line 2 but points out to would-be rulers that in this way they lose their chance to be "lord" (or "ruler"—*chün*) of the whole land.

Text A is essentially the same as Text B—though more on this below. In line 3, Text A is like the standard text in having "does not become parted from (*li*) his luggage," where Text B has "get far away from (*yüan*)."

The Ma-wang-tui texts have "Therefore the *gentleman*" (*chün-tzu*) in line 3 where the standard text has "Therefore the Sage" (*sheng-jen*); this is a common variant. And in line 5 the Ma-wang-tui texts have "the king of . . ." (*wang*) where later texts all have "the ruler of . . ." (*chu*).

The addition of several grammatical particles in lines 4 and 5, and a slight change in wording in 4, greatly clarify what these lines are intended to say. The standard text, translated by Wing-tsit Chan, reads as follows: "Even at the sight of magnificent scenes, He remains leisurely and indifferent. How is it that a lord with ten thousand chariots Should behave lightheartedly in his empire?"[143] For "magnificent scenes" (*jung-kuan*) the Ma-wang-tui texts have—it appears—"walled-in hostel" (*huan-kuan*), and grammatically the line, at least in Text A, follows the pattern "only when you have X condition, do you then have Y result."[144]

The added particle *yü* ("than") in line 5 shows us that two things are being compared—that is, the wise king will not look upon his own person as less important *than* the whole land. The standard text lacks this *yü*.

[B]

重爲輕根靜爲趮君是以君子冬日行

不遠示畱重雖有環官燕處則昭若〓

何萬乘之王而以身輕於天下輕則失

本趮則失君

[A]

□爲巠根清爲趮君是以君子衆日行

不離其甾重唯有環官燕處□□若〓

何萬乘之王而以身巠於天下巠則失

本趮則失君

[CHAPTER 27]

1 The good traveler leaves no track behind;
2 The good speaker [speaks] without blemish or flaw;
3 The good counter doesn't use tallies or chips;
4 The good closer of doors does so without bolt or lock, and yet the door cannot be opened;
5 The good tier of knots ties without rope or cord, yet his knots can't be undone.

6 Therefore the Sage is constantly good at saving men and never rejects anyone;
7 And with things, he never rejects useful goods.
8 This is called Doubly Bright.

9 Therefore the good man is the teacher of the good,
10 And the bad man is the raw material for the good.
11 To not value one's teacher and not cherish the raw goods—
12 Though one had great knowledge, he would still be greatly confused.
13 This is called the Essential of the Sublime.

COMMENTS AND NOTES

In line 12, Text A has "greatly *blind*" where Text B (in agreement with later texts) has "greatly *confused*." Line 4 in Text B actually begins, "The good *counter (shu)* and closer of doors." But it seems clear that the copyist mistakenly started to copy line 3 again.

The Ma-wang-tui texts have a number of variant characters in the opening lines (1–5), but they do not substantially affect the meaning.

In line 6 the Ma-wang-tui texts have "*and* never rejects anyone" *(erh)* where the standard reading is "and *therefore* never rejects anyone" *(ku)*. Line 7 in the standard text simply repeats line 6, starting from "constantly good at," substituting "things" *(wu)* for "men" *(jen)*. Wing-tsit Chan translates the two lines, "Therefore the sage is always good in saving men and consequently no man is rejected; He is always good in saving things and consequently nothing is rejected."[145]

In line 9 later texts all say the exact opposite of what is said here—namely, "Therefore the good man is the teacher of the bad man."

善行者无䟆迹□言者无瑕適善數者
不以檮筭善閉者无闗籥而不可啓也
善結者□□約□而不可解也□是以
聲人恒善伏人而无棄人物无棄財□
是胃忡明故善□□□之師不善人善
人之齎也□不貴其師不愛其齎唯知
乎大眯是胃眇要

善行者无迹迹善言者无瑕適善數者
不用梯筭善○閉者无關籥而不可啓
也善結者无繩約而不可解也是以耶
人恒善俅人而无棄人物无棄財是胃
曳明故善〓人〓之師不善人善人之
資也不貴亓師不愛亓資雖知乎大迷
是胃眇要

1 When you know the male yet hold on to the female,
2 You'll be the ravine of the country.
3 When you're the ravine of the country,
4 Your constant virtue will not leave.
5 And when your constant virtue doesn't leave,
6 You'll return *to* **the state of the infant.**

7 **When you know** the pure yet hold on to the soiled,
8 You'll be the valley of the country.
9 When you're the valley of the country,
10 Your constant virtue is complete.
11 And when your constant virtue is complete,
12 You'll return to the state of uncarved wood.

13 When you know the white yet hold on to the black,
14 You'll be the model for the country.
15 And when you're the model for the country,
16 Your constant virtue will not go astray,
17 And when your constant virtue does not go astray,
18 You'll return to the condition which has no limit.

19 When uncarved wood is cut up, it's turned into vessels;
20 When the Sage is used, he becomes the Head of Officials.
21 Truly, great carving is done without splitting up.

COMMENTS AND NOTES

Texts A and B are essentially the same. The copyist of Text A incorrectly omitted the word "white" in line 13; and in lines 8 and 9 the B copyist, looking ahead to the start of line 10, mistakenly wrote in "constant" (*heng*) before the word "valley" (*ku*, but here *yü*).

One small grammatical change in line 20 makes clear the parallel structure of lines 19 and 20 and clarifies what those lines mean. In most other editions of the *Lao-tzu*, in line 20 we are told—"When the Sage uses it" (*yung-chih*); here it says when he "is used" (*yung*). Wing-tsit Chan translates the standard text: "When the uncarved wood is broken up, it is turned into concrete things. But when the sage uses it, he becomes the leading official."[146]

Lines 19–21 play with double meanings throughout. The word for "vessel" (*ch'i*) can mean a government lackey; it refers to someone who is technically specialized, but one who lacks the all-around vir-

[B]

知亓雄守亓雌爲＝天＝下＝鷄＝恒＝
德＝不＝离＝復＝□□□＝亓白
守亓辱爲＝天＝下＝浴＝○恒＝德＝
乃＝足＝復＝歸於樸知亓白守亓黑
爲＝天＝下＝式＝恒＝德＝不＝貸
復＝歸於无極樸散則爲器耵人用則
爲官長夫大制无割

[A]

知其雄守其雌爲＝天＝下＝鷄＝恒＝
德＝不＝鷄＝復＝歸嬰兒知其白守其
辱乙爲＝天＝下＝浴＝恒＝
□知其守其黑爲＝天＝下＝乃＝
式＝恒＝德＝不＝貸＝復＝歸於无極乙
樸散□□□人用則爲官長夫大制
无割

tue and talent of the "gentleman." (In *Analects* 2:12, Confucius says, "The Gentleman is not a vessel.") Then in line 21 "carving" or "cutting" (*chih*) also means "regulating" in a governmental way; that is, the Sage is someone who will govern (=carve) without destroying (=splitting up) what is genuine and natural in people.

Lines 5, 11, and 17 are omitted in the standard text. And, in the standard text, stanzas 2 and 3 (i.e., lines 7–12, and 13–18) are reversed. The standard order allows for better continuity, moving directly from the "uncarved wood" (*p'u*) of line 12 to the "uncarved wood" of line 19. But it is possible that lines 19–21 were originally intended to be read as a unit with lines 1–6 in chapter 29, and that stanzas 2 and 3 of 28 were reversed only after these two chapters assumed their present form.147

[CHAPTER 29]

1   For those who would like to take control of the world and act on it—
2   I see that with this they simply will not succeed.
3   The world is a sacred vessel;
4   It is not something that can be acted upon.
5   Those who act on it destroy it;
6   Those who hold on to it lose it.

7   With things—some go forward, others follow;
8   Some are hot, others submissive and weak;
9   Some rise up while others fall down.
10 Therefore the Sage:
11 Rejects the extreme, the excessive, and the extravagant.

COMMENTS AND NOTES

In Text A there is a lacuna in the text running from the "others" of line 8 to the beginning of line 9, but the reconstruction of the text shows not one character missing ("submissive and weak") but five. Thus Text A appears to have been in agreement with later editions of the *Lao-tzu* in having four pairs of "somes-and-others" at the end of chapter 29.

I find Hsü K'ang-sheng's discussion of these lines persuasive (Hsü, 1985, pp. 120–121): he feels that the missing characters should be *ch'ui huo ch'iang huo ts'o*—"blow cold, some are firm and strong, others submissive and weak," thus giving, starting with line 8, "Some are hot, others blow cold; some are firm and strong, others submissive and weak." (This is essentially the reading we find in the Fu I text.) It seems clear that throughout we have pairs of extremes.

Wing-tsit Chan's translation of the standard text here is, "Among creatures some lead and some follow. Some blow hot and some blow cold. Some are strong and some are weak. Some may break and some may fall.[148]

[A]

將欲取天下而爲之吾見其弗□□
□□器也非可爲者也爲者敗之執
者失之物或行或隨或炅或□□□
□或坏或擖是以聲人去甚去大去楮

[B]

將欲取□□□□□□□□□得已夫
天下神器也非可爲者也爲之者敗之
執之者失之○物或行或隋或熱或硓
或陪或墮是以耶人去甚去大去諸

[CHAPTER 30]

1 Those who assist their rulers with the Way,
2 Don't use weapons to commit violence in the world.
3 Such *deeds easily rebound.*
4 **In places where** *armies* **are stationed, thorns** and brambles will grow.
5 The good [general] achieves his result and that's all;
6 He does not use the occasion to seize strength from it.

7 He achieves his result but does not become arrogant;
8 He achieves his result but does not praise his deeds;
9 He achieves his result **and yet** *does not* brag.
10 He achieves his result, yet he abides with the result because he has no choice.[149]
11 This is called achieving one's result [**without**] using force.

12 When things reach their prime, they get old;
13 We call this "not the Way."
14 What is not the Way will come to an early end.

COMMENTS AND NOTES

On lines 12–14, see the comments and notes to chapter 55, above.

In line 11, Text A agrees with the standard text in saying "without using force" (or "while not being strong"—*pu-ch'iang*). The omission of the negative *pu* in Text B seems to be a mistake.

The standard text adds a line after line 4—"Great wars are always followed by famines."[150] The line is also missing from a few other texts and has been suspected for some time as being commentary on the previous line.

In the standard text, line 9 comes before 7 and 8. Also, line 10 in the standard text is "He achieves his purpose but only as an unavoidable step"[151] (*pu-te-i*); the Ma-wang-tui texts have *wu-te-i chü*, the *chü* that means "to dwell" or "reside." My translation is tentative: the line might also mean (reading the final *i* here as the instrumental *i*) "He achieves his purpose and yet cannot because of this dwell on it." *Chü* as "to dwell" seems to mean "excessively dwelling on one's accomplishments" in chapter 2 and elsewhere.

The standard text omits the words "this is called" (*shih-wei*) at the start of line 11, but a number of texts agree with the Ma-wang-tui texts in having this addition; some texts also just say "this."

[A]

以道佐人主不以兵強□天下□□
□□所居楚朸生之善者果而已矣
毋以取強焉∠果而毋驕∠
∠果而□果而毋得已居是胃□而
不強物壯而老是胃之不□道□蚤
已

[B]

以道佐人主不以兵強於天下□元□
□□□□□棘生之善者果而已矣
毋以取焉焉毋毋驕果而勿矜果□
□伐果而毋得已居是胃果而強物壯
而老胃之不□道□蚤已∠

In his translation of the standard text of *Lao-tzu*, D. C. Lau puts lines 7–11 all in the imperative mode (e.g., "bring it to a conclusion but do not boast"[152]), but he has softened this interpretation in his translation of the Ma-wang-tui texts. He now has "He should be resolute but must not be arrogant; he should be resolute but must not brag about it,"[153] and so on. In an earlier study, I treated these *wu*'s as imperative.[154]

[CHAPTER 31, *TEXT A*]

1 As for weapons—they **are** instruments of ill omen.
2 And among things there are those that hate them.
3 Therefore, the one who has the Way, with them does not dwell.
4 When the gentleman is at home, he honors the left;
5 When at war, he honors the right.
6 Therefore, weapons are not the instrument of the gentleman—
7 **Weapons** are instruments of ill omen.
8 When you have no choice but to use them, it's best to remain tranquil and calm.
9 You should never look upon them as things of beauty.
10 If you see them as beautiful things—this is to delight in the killing of men.
11 And when you delight in the killing of men, you'll not realize your goal in the land.

12 Therefore, in happy events we honor the left,
13 But in mourning we honor the right.
14 Therefore, the lieutenant general stands on the left;
15 And the supreme general stands on the right.
16 Which is to say, they arrange themselves as they would at a funeral.
17 When multitudes of people are killed, we stand before them in sorrow and grief.
18 When we're victorious in battle, we treat the occasion like a funeral ceremony.

COMMENTS AND NOTES

Text B is essentially the same as Text A. Now missing from Text B are lines 3 and 13, part of line 12 and most of line 17.

In line 1, the standard text opens with "As for *fine/beautiful* weapons"; the word "fine" (*chia*) does not occur in the Ma-wang-tui texts.

Line 3 literally says, "Therefore *one who has desires* . . ." (*yu-yū che*), not "Therefore one who has the Way . . ." (in Text A; Text B has a lacuna at this point). I think this is a mistake; see my comment above on the same line in chapter 24.

The "Therefore" at the start of line 6 in the Ma-wang-tui texts does not occur in the standard text; also, in the standard text, lines 6 and 7 are reversed.

[A]

夫兵者不祥之器□物或惡之∠故有
欲者弗居君子居則貴左用兵則貴右
∠故兵者非君子之器也□□不祥之
器也不得已而之銛襲爲上勿美也
若美之是樂殺人也夫樂殺人不可以
得志於天下矣∠是以吉事上左∠喪
事上右∠是以便將軍居左上將軍居
右言以喪禮居之也殺人衆以悲依立
之戰勝以喪禮處之

[B]

夫兵者不祥之器也物或亞□□□
□□□子居則貴左用兵者不祥□
器也不
兵者非君子之器也不
得已而用之銛憺爲上勿美也若美之
是樂殺人也夫樂殺人不可以得志於
天下矣是以吉事□□□□□□是以
偏將軍居左而上將軍居右言以喪禮
居之也殺□□□□□□立□朕而以
喪禮處之

Line 9 in the standard text is somewhat different. In place of the brief "do not beautify it [or them]" (*wu mei yeh*), we have, rather, "defeat and yet not see as beauty" (*sheng erh pu mei*). Wing-tsit Chan's translation reads, "Even when he is victorious he does not regard it as praiseworthy."155 But the Ma-wang-tui form of this line is attested in other editions.

The "Therefore" at the head of line 12 does not occur in the standard text, but it is a known variant. The same is true for the "Therefore" at the head of line 14.

In the standard text the "mourning" (*sang*) of line 13 has been changed to "bad fortune" *(hsiung)* to directly contrast with the "good fortune" (my "happy"—*chi*) of line 12.

Finally, at the end of line 17 the standard text has "weep" instead of "stand" (i.e., *ch'i* instead of *li*). Chou Tz'u-chi,[156] Hsü K'ang-sheng,[157] and D. C. Lau[158] all read *ch'i* as the *li* that means "to come" or "to arrive." I see no reason not to read the character as it stands, though any of the suggested alternatives makes equally good sense of the line.

Chapter 31 is one of two chapters in the *Lao-tzu* (the other one being 66) that was not commented on by Wang Pi (A.D. 226–249). D. C. Lau points out that "this fact has been variously interpreted. Some think that this means that this chapter is a late interpolation. Others think that Wang's commentary has become mixed up with the text. Still others think that this means at least that Wang suspected the authenticity of the chapter and showed this by leaving it without commentary."[159] Clearly, the chapter already existed in its present form at the start of the Han dynasty.

It is also worth noting that in some editions of the *Lao-tzu* chapters 30 and 31 are combined since both deal with similar themes.[160]

CHAPTER 32

1 The Tao is constantly nameless.
2 Though in its natural state it seems small, no one in the world dares to treat it as a subject.
3 Were marquises and kings able to maintain it,
4 The ten thousand things would submit to them on their own,
5 And Heaven and Earth would unite to send forth sweet dew.
6 By nature it would fall equally on all things, **with no one among the people** ordering that it be so.

7 As soon as we start to establish a system, we have names.
8 And as soon as there are set names,
9 Then you must <u>also</u> know that it's time to stop.
10 By knowing to stop—in this way you'll come to no harm.
11 **The Way's presence in the world**
12 Is like the relationship of small valley [streams] to rivers and seas.

COMMENTS AND NOTES

There is very little left of Text A (missing are portions of lines 2, 6, 8, 9, 10, 11, and 12); from what survives, Text A seems to have been exactly the same as Text B (with the exception of a few insignificant character variants).

The differences between the Ma-wang-tui form of this chapter and that found in the standard text are all minor. In line 2 the standard text has "no one *is able* to treat it as subject" versus "no one *dares*." In line 5, where the Ma-wang-tui texts have "send forth" (*yū*) sweet dew, other editions of the *Lao-tzu* say, "send down" (*chiang*). And finally, in line 10, the standard text says that by knowing to stop you "can" (*k'o-i*) avoid harm versus "in this way" (*so-i*) you'll come to no harm.

My "natural state" in line 2 is literally *p'u*, "natural, uncarved, wood," and D. C. Lau picks up the echo in this chapter from the end of chapter 28, where "carving" natural wood corresponds to establishing government regulations and we are told that "great carving [=great establishing—*chih*] in a governmental way" is done without destroying what is natural in people. The same *chih* occurs here in line 7, which D. C. Lau translates, "Then only when it is cut are there names."[161]

[A]

也

道恒无名□樸唯□□□□□□□
王若能守之萬物將自賓天地相谷以
俞甘洛〻民莫之□□〻玙焉始制有
□□□□有夫□□〻所以不
□俾道之在天□□□□浴之與江海

[B]

道恒无名樸唯小而天下弗敢臣侯王
若能守之萬物將自賓天地相合以俞
甘洛□□□令而自均焉始制有名〻
亦既有夫亦將知〻止〻所以不殆卑
□在天下也猷小浴之與江海也

[261]

CHAPTER 33

1 To understand others is to be knowledgeable;
2 To understand yourself is to be wise.
3 To conquer others is to have strength;
4 To conquer yourself is to be strong.
5 To know when you have enough is to be rich.
6 To go forward with strength is to have ambition.
7 To not lose your place is to last long.
8 To die but not be forgotten—that's [true] long life.

COMMENTS AND NOTES

What remains of Text A is exactly the same as Text B; missing are portions of lines 2 and 3 and all of line 5.

The grammatical *yeh* at the end of each line in the Ma-wang-tui texts, signaling the equative sentence pattern (X, Y *yeh* = X is Y), adds strength to the interpretation of these lines as definitions, but reading the lines as "the one who" sentences (e.g., "The one who understands others is knowledgeable") is still possible.

Significantly, the Ma-wang-tui texts have *wang* ("to forget /be forgotten") in the last line where other editions of the text have *wang* ("to perish"). The standard reading is "To die but not really perish—that's [true] long life." The question then becomes, what does it mean to "perish"? Since the only difference between the two characters is that the heart radical is added to the character meaning "to perish" to give us *wang* ("to forget"), it is possible that even with the character "to forget" the author intends the meaning "to perish." But "to die but not be forgotten" forms a good definition of "true long life," and the author of the chapter is intent throughout in giving us new meanings for certain words.[162]

While it seems clear that lines 2 and 4 are meant to contrast with lines 1 and 3, it is not clear how lines 5–8 relate to one another. I have decided to read all four lines as lines that stand alone and define for us positive things; that is, this is what it really means, in a good Taoist way, to "be rich," "have ambition," "last long," and "live a long life." (The author clearly should have added a line between lines 4 and 5 that would contrast with what follows, something like "To have money is to have wealth," but "To know when you have enough is to be rich.")

Arthur Waley contrasts lines 6 and 7: "He that works through

[A]

知人者知也自知□□□□者有力
也自勝者□□□□□也／强行者
有志也不失其所者久也死不忘者**壽**
也

[B]

知人者知也自知也明也朕人者有力也
自朕者强也知足者富也强行者有志
也不失亓所者久也死而不忘者**壽**也

---

violence may get his way; But only what stays in its place can endure."[163] My guess would be that the author in line 6 is putting forth a good way to have ambition as opposed to what that normally means (i.e., to strive for fame and glory); line 7 might mean that to really last long, the key is to know and accept one's lot in life.

CHAPTER 34

1 The Way floats and drifts;
2 It can go left or right.
3 It accomplishes its tasks and completes **its affairs, and yet** for this it is not given a name.
4 The ten thousand things entrust their lives to it, and yet it does not act as their master.
5 Thus it is constantly without desires.
6 It can be named with the things that are small.
7 The ten thousand things entrust their lives to it, and yet it does not act as their master.
8 It can be named with the things that are great.

9   Therefore the Sage's ability to accomplish the great
10 Comes from his not playing the role of the great.
11 Therefore he is able to accomplish the great.

COMMENTS AND NOTES

In Text A there is a lacuna between "The Way" in line 1 and "completes its affairs" in line 3. Otherwise, Text A and Text B are essentially the same.

Note how line 5 seems out of place; it interrupts what is otherwise the nice parallelism of lines 4 and 6 with lines 7 and 8. The point is that for one and the same reason (that it does not act as the master of things) the Way is both small (i.e., seemingly insignificant and unknown) and large (or great, *ta*). The Sage-ruler should take this as his model.

In the standard text of *Lao-tzu* the text differs in a number of ways. To begin with, a line is added between lines 2 and 3, the line that Chan translates, "All things depend on it for life, and it does not turn away from them."[164] Secondly, at the start of line 4, in place of the very nice words "It clothes and nourishes the ten thousand things" (*i-yang wan-wu*), the Ma-wang-tui texts have "The ten thousand things entrust their lives to it." Thirdly, the words "completes its affairs" are omitted from line 3 in the standard text. And finally, lines 9–11 are phrased somewhat differently in the standard text; they are less redundant than they are here. (Chan translates, "Therefore [the Sage] never strives himself for the great, and thereby the great is achieved."[165])

[B]

道渢呵亓可左右也成功遂□□弗名

有也萬物歸焉而弗爲主則恒无欲也

可名於小萬物歸焉而弗爲主可命於

大是以耵人之能成大也以亓不爲大

也故能成大

[A]

道汎□□□□□□□□遂事而弗名

有也萬物歸焉而弗爲主則恒无欲也

可名於小萬物歸焉□□爲主可名於

大∠是□聲人之能成大也以其不爲

大也故能成大

CHAPTER 35

1 Hold on to the Great Image and the whole world will come to you.

2 Come to you and suffer no harm; but rather know great safety and peace.

3 Music and **food**—for these passing travelers stop.

4 Therefore, of the Tao's speaking, we say:

5 Insipid, it is! It's lack of flavor.

6 When you look at it, it's not sufficient to be seen;

7 When you listen to it, it's not sufficient to be heard;

8 Yet when you use it, it can't be used up.

COMMENTS AND NOTES

Texts A and B are the same.

Chou Tz'u-chi speculates that the Ma-wang-tui *ko* at the end of line 3 (which he reads as "correct" or "proper") might be the right word here instead of the common "traveler" or "guest" *(k'o)*.[166] In that case the line would read, "When music and food go beyond what is proper, you should stop."

The only significant difference between the Ma-wang-tui texts and later editions is in the syntax of line 4. The Ma-wang-tui "Therefore" *(ku)* at the head of the line is not found in other texts, nor is the "we say" *(yüeh)* at the end.

[B]

執大象天下往＝ 而不害安平大樂與
□過格止故道之出言也曰淡呵亓无
味也視之不足見也聽之不足聞也用
之不可既也

[A]

執大象□□往＝ 而不害安平大乙樂
與餌過格止故道之出言也曰談呵其
无味也□□不足見也聽之不足聞也
用之不可既也

CHAPTER 36

1 If you wish to shrink it,
2 You must certainly stretch it.
3 If you wish to weaken it,
4 You must certainly strengthen it.
5 If you wish to desert it,
6 You must certainly work closely with it.
7 If you wish to snatch something from it,
8 You must certainly give something to it.
9 This is called the Subtle Light.
10 The submissive and weak conquer the strong.

11 Fish should not be taken out of the depths;
12 The state's sharp weapons should not be shown to the people.

COMMENTS AND NOTES

Texts A and B are the same: the different characters in the two seem to intend the same word.

In line 5 the Ma-wang-tui texts have "leave" or "desert" *(ch'ü)* where other editions of the *Lao-tzu* have "reject/throw away" *(fei)*, and to match that, in line 6 the Ma-wang-tui texts have "work closely with it" or "share with it" *(yü)* where later editions all have "promote" or "elevate" *(hsing)*. In line 8 the Ma-wang-tui texts use one character for "give to it" *(yü)*, the standard text uses another—the *yü* which is used in line 6 of the Ma-wang-tui texts with the meaning of "share."

[B]

將欲擒之必古張之將欲弱之必古○
強之將欲去之必古與之將欲奪之必
古予□是胃微明柔弱朕强魚不可說
於淵國利器不可以示人

[A]

將欲拾之必古張之將欲弱之必□□强
之將欲去之必古與之∠將欲奪之必
古予之是胃微明∠∠弱勝强魚不脫
於瀟邦利器不可以視人∠

[CHAPTER 37]

1 The Tao is constantly nameless.
2 Were marquises and kings able to maintain it,
3 The ten thousand things would transform on their own.
4 Having transformed, were their desires to become active,
5 I would subdue them with the nameless simplicity.
6 Having subdued them with the nameless simplicity,
7 I would not disgrace them.
8 By not being disgraced, they will be tranquil.
9 And Heaven and Earth will of themselves be correct and right.

10 The Way—2,426 [characters]

COMMENTS AND NOTES

The "able" in line 2 is omitted in Text A: line 2 in Text A would read, "If marquises and kings maintain it." Line 10 does not occur in Text A.

Line 1 in the standard text is "Tao invariably takes no action, and yet there is nothing left undone."[167] This is one of two places in the standard text—the other one being chapter 48—where the phrase *wu-wei erh wu pu-wei*, "does nothing and yet there is nothing left undone," occurs (in some editions of the text the phrase is also found in chapters 3 and 38). Line 1 is quite different in the Ma-wang-tui texts; in fact lines 1, 2, and 3 here are virtually identical to lines 1, 3, and 4 in chapter 32.

The line *wu-wei erh wu pu-wei* is also missing in chapter 48 in the Ma-wang-tui texts. This has prompted a number of scholars to argue that this idea was not originally part of the philosophy of the author. It was added later, they feel, under the influence of Legalist thought (where it normally means that the ruler leaves all day-to-day business to his ministers, and thus everything gets done even though he himself does not act). But I have pointed out elsewhere that it is not that the line did not occur in chapter 48 of the Ma-wang-tui texts; rather, there is a lacuna in both texts at this point, and the missing spaces seem to indicate that the line *was* originally there.[168] Also, the end of chapter 3, without necessarily using these exact words, says much the same thing— "If he [the Sage] can bring it about that those without knowledge simply do not dare to act, Then there is nothing that will not be in order."

The words "Having subdued them with" (*chen-chih i*) are omit-

[B]

道恒无名侯王若能守之萬物將自化
=而欲作吾將闐=之=以=无=名
=之=樸=夫將不=辱=以靜天地
將自正　道　二千四百廿六

[A]

道恒无名／侯王若守之萬物將自愙
=而欲□□□□□之以无=名
=之=楃=夫將不=辱=以情天地
將自正

---

ted from the beginning of line 6 in the standard text; and in lines 7 and 8, the standard text has "not desire" *(pu-yü)* where the Ma-wang-tui texts have "not disgrace" *(pu-ju)*. Thus the standard text for lines 6–8 has, as Wing-tsit Chan translates, "Simplicity, which has no name, is free of desires. Being free of desires, it is tranquil."[169]

Finally, in line 9, the standard text has "the world" *(t'ien-hsia)* where the Ma-wang-tui texts have "Heaven and Earth" *(t'ien-ti),* and "at peace" or "settled" *(ting)* in place of "correct and right" *(cheng).*

ADDITIONAL NOTES

1. There is an official biography of Lao-tzu, or Li Erh, in Ssu-ma Ch'ien's first great history of the Chinese people, the *Shih-chi* (Historical Records), compiled c. 100 B.C.; that biography is translated into English by Wing-tsit Chan (1963, pp. 36–37). But as Chan's review of the scholarship on this biography (pp. 37–59) shows, many scholars are convinced that this does little in terms of identifying the actual author of the text. For an excellent study of where the data in this biography come from and how this identity of Lao-tzu came to be, see A. C. Graham's article "The Origins of the Legend of Lao Tan" (Graham, 1986). Also useful on the problem of the authorship of this text is appendix 1 to D. C. Lau's translation, "The Problem of Authorship" (Lau, 1963, pp. 147–62).

2. There are two good translations of the *Chuang-tzu*, one by Burton Watson (Watson, 1968), the other by A. C. Graham (Graham, 1981). The Watson translation is superior in terms of literary quality; the Graham translation is more astute in drawing attention to the philosophical concepts developed by Chuang-tzu.

3. For an excellent summary of these textual finds, see Michael Loewe's article (Loewe, 1977). Part of the Ch'in law code is translated and discussed by Katrina McLeod and Robin Yates (McLeod and Yates, 1981). On this law code see also A.F.P. Hulsewé's translation, *Remnants of Ch'in Law* and Yates' review of it, "Some Notes on Ch'in Law: A Review Article of *Remnants of Ch'in Law* by A.F.P. Hulsewé."

4. For more on this point, see the article by William Boltz (Boltz, 1985).

5. For more detail on the texts discovered at Ma-wang-tui, see "Ma-wang-tui" (Henricks, 1986), pp. 614–17.

6. Later texts also change *ch'i* ("to open") to *k'ai* (also "to open") to avoid using the personal name of Emperor Ching (r. 156–141 B.C.), Liu Ch'i, and they change the negative *fu* ("not

[verb] it") to *pu* ("not [verb]") to avoid the personal name of Emperor Chao of the Han (r. 86–74 B.C.), Liu Fu-ling.

7. The text is not called the *Lao-tzu*, nor is it called the *Tao-te ching*. At the end of part II, Text B has the notation "Virtue—3,041 [characters]," and at the end of part I it has "The Way—2,426 [characters]." The notations "Virtue" and "The Way" probably indicate no more than the fact that chapter 38 begins with the phrase "Virtue" ("the highest virtue," *shang-te*) while chapter 1 begins with the word "Way" (*tao*). It was common practice in early China to use the first word or words of a section of text as its title.

For more on the total number of characters in the text, see my article "The Ma-wang-tui Texts of *Lao-tzu* and Lines of Textual Transmission" (Henricks, 1985).

8. See their article "Shih t'an Ma-wang-tui Han-mu chung ti po-shu *Lao-tzu*" (Kao and Ch'ih, 1974) and my study "Examining the Ma-wang-tui Silk Texts of the *Lao-tzu*" (Henricks, 1979a). Actually the author of the "Explaining *Lao-tzu*" chapter skips around in his treatment of the text of *Lao-tzu*, discussing chapters in the sequence 38, 58, 59, 60, 46, 14, 1, 50, 67, 53, and 54.

9. See Yen Ling-feng, *Ma-wang-tui po-shu Lao-tzu shih-t'an* (Yen, 1976), pp. 8–13.

10. There are eighteen such "periods" in all. They occur at the start of line 1 in chapter 46, at the start of line 3 in chapter 46, at the start of line 1 in chapter 51, at the start of line 6 in chapter 51, at the start of line 5 in chapter 52, at the start of line 1 in chapter 53, at the start of line 1 in chapter 57, at the start of line 1 in chapter 63, at the start of line 1 in chapter 64, at the start of line 1 in chapter 80, at the start of line 7 in chapter 81, at the start of line 1 in chapter 69, at the start of line 2 in chapter 72, at the start of line 1 in chapter 73, at the start of line 1 in chapter 75, at the start of line 7 in chapter 75, at the start of line 1 in chapter 76, and at the start of line 1 in chapter 1. There are also what appear to be "commas" (,) on occasion at the ends of phrases and lines in both texts (though mostly in Text A), and repetition of a character or phrase is often indicated in the Ma-wang-tui texts by what are apparently ditto marks; they follow the word or phrase to be repeated and look like equals signs (=).

11. Henricks, 1982.

12. That is, it is Yang times Yang ($9 \times 9 = 81$). Yin times Yang (8×9), or 72, is also a magical number. Confucius is often said to have had seventy-two disciples.

13. For the distinction Lao-tzu makes between "name" and "style" in chapter 25, see my "Comments and Notes" to this chapter below.

14. Chan, 1963, p. 160.

15. This analogy was first developed in "The Tao and the Field: Exploring an Analogy" (Henricks, 1981d).

16. But see the "Comments and Notes" to chapter 37 on this phrase in the Ma-wang-tui texts.

17. The analogy of the "Tao and the Field" is not perfect, and one of the ways in which it does not work is that the analogy would seem to suggest a view of periodic creation of the world; that is, every so often the entire world of things comes into being and then the cosmos passes through distinct stages of growth, maturity, decline, and death (i.e., the four seasons), followed again by rebirth (in the manner of the *kalpas* of Indian cosmology). The Taoists treat creation as a once-and-for-all thing, even though it is true that in some way all distinct things that live and die "return" to the Tao and each new thing "comes from" the Tao as well.

18. Despite the fact that it is difficult to talk about the philosophy of Lao-tzu without using the words "who people are by nature," the word *hsing* ("human nature," "inborn nature") does not occur in the text of the *Lao-tzu* and occurs only rarely in the "Inner Chapters" of the *Chuang-tzu*. Taoist ideas about "human nature" *are* developed in what A. C. Graham identifies as the "Primitivist" chapters of the *Chuang-tzu* (chapters 8–10 and the first part of 11) and also in the *Huai-nan tzu* (on which see Roth, 1985). When they talk about human nature, Taoists tend to emphasize the ways in which people *differ* by nature (unique talents and personality traits), whereas the Confucians tend to concentrate on the ways in which people are all the same (shared innate moral traits). Note also the article by Isabelle Robinet, "La notion de *hsing* dans le taoïsme et son rapport avec celle du confucianisme" (Robinet, 1986).

19. See his article, "The *Nung-chia* 'School of the Tillers' and the Origins of Peasant Utopianism in China" (Graham, 1986), p. 82. The Tillers believed there should be a ruler of the state but that he would do very little other than regulate and maintain agricultural policy. He, too, should grow his own food and weave his own clothes, as should every family.

20. Max Kaltenmark (Kaltenmark, 1970, pp. 85–98) presents Chuang-tzu as a thoroughgoing mystic and teacher of meditation and

ecstasy-producing techniques. I take issue with this view; I think it misrepresents the Chuang-tzu we meet in the text.

21. See the "Comments and Notes" to chapter 16, below, on the Ma-wang-tui form of lines 1 and 2.

22. Translation by Burton Watson (Watson, 1968), pp. 57–58. Note that both "mind fasting" and "sitting in forgetfulness" *(tso-wang),* a meditative procedure described in chapter 6 of the *Chuang-tzu,* are taken up into the Taoist religion as important kinds of meditation. On this point see Livia Köhn's recent study (Köhn, 1987).

23. On *śamatha-vipaśyanā* in the Fa-hsiang School of Chinese Buddhism see, for example, Alan Sponberg, "Meditation in Fa-hsiang Buddhism" (Sponberg, 1986). Note that it is also this *kuan* that I translate as "perceive" and "see" in lines 5 and 6 of chapter 1: "Therefore, those constantly without desires, by this means will perceive its subtlety. Those constantly with desires, by this means will see only that which they yearn for and seek."

24. Thus the verse on enlightenment that is attributed to Shen-hsiu by his opponents in the Southern School is, "The body is the Bodhi tree, The mind is like a clear mirror. At all times we must strive to polish it, And must not let the dust collect" (tr. by Philip B. Yampolsky [Yampolsky, 1967, p. 130]). For the first thorough study in English of Shen-hsiu and the Northern School see John R. McRae's recent book (McRae, 1986).

25. On this practice, see Andersen, 1979.

26. Maspero's detailed study of these breathing techniques remains our main source of information. His article is translated into English as "Methods of 'Nourishing the Vital Principle' in the Ancient Taoist Religion" (book IX, pp. 445–554, in Maspero, 1981).

27. It is worth noting that *wei,* "action," means, in Chinese philosophical parlance, the action one takes after consciously deliberating the alternatives, and contrasts, therefore, with action as natural, un-thought-out response. The philosopher Hsün-tzu (born c. 312 B.C.) contrasts "nature" or "natural response" *(hsing)* with "conscious activity" *(wei)* in this way: "That which is harmonious from birth, which is capable of perceiving through the senses and of responding to stimulus spontaneously and without effort, is . . . called the nature. . . . When the emotions are aroused and the mind makes a choice from among them, this is called thought. When the mind conceives a thought and the body puts it into action, this is called conscious activity" (tr. by Burton Watson [Watson, 1963, pp. 139–40]).

I disagree with Herrlee Creel's understanding of *wu-wei* in the *Lao-tzu*, which equates it with the Legalist notion in which the ruler "does not act" because he leaves all matters of administrative detail to his officials. Nonetheless, his article can still be read with benefit. See his "On the Origins of *Wu-wei*," in Creel, 1970, pp. 48–78.

28.   In chapter 38 Lao-tzu seems to rank the Confucian virtues, with humanity (or "benevolence"—the highest of the Confucian virtues) being the highest, righteousness next, and propriety last. We might speculate that Lao-tzu understands humanity as moral action that stems from genuine concern for the welfare of others; righteousness as action done simply because it is the "right" thing to do (not necessarily because one genuinely wants to do it); and propriety as action done not necessarily because it is "right" but purely because it is thought to be "proper." Note that "virtue" in chapter 38 is seen to be superior to even the supreme Confucian virtue of humanity in that people of humanity still take action *(wei)* even though they have no reason for acting this way, whereas people of true virtue do not act *(wu-wei*—i.e., they act spontaneously, without deliberation and intention) but they have no reason for acting this way.

29.   Note that the line in chapter 19 that says people will *return* to filial piety if the notions of humanity and righteousness are abandoned seems to indicate that Lao-tzu believed that people left on their own would be good, to a degree at least, "by nature." That filial piety is a given in human nature might have also been part of Chuang-tzu's view. In chapter 4 of the *Chuang-tzu*, Confucius—here surely voicing Chuang-tzu's own view—says, "In the world, there are two great decrees: one is fate and the other is duty. That a son should love his parents is fate—you cannot erase this from his heart. That a subject should serve his ruler is duty—there is no place he can go and be without his ruler, no place he can escape to between heaven and earth." (Watson, 1968, pp. 59–60.)

30.   That wealth and fame could damage one's chances for long life is something with which later Taoists who "nourished" their lives agreed. See, for example, Hsi K'ang's (A.D. 223–262) essays on "nourishing life" in Henricks, 1983, pp. 21–70.

31.   A. C. Graham argues that living out one's natural years in happiness and health was a concern shared by the Taoists and the "Individualists" or "Yangists," the followers of the philosopher Yang Chu, in ancient China (see pp. 9–17 of his article "The Background of the Mencian Theory of Human Nature" [Graham, 1986], and pp. 221–23 in Graham, 1981). But the Yangists felt this end would be

achieved only by means of careful, deliberate calculation, whereas the Taoists favored spontaneity and unconcern as the means to the end.

32. Some of the most delightful things that Chuang-tzu says are things he says about death, where he speculates on what it *might* be and what will follow. See what he says in chapters 2, 6, and 18 (pp. 47, 80, 83–85, and 191–92, respectively, in Watson, 1968).

33. Translation by Burton Watson (Watson, 1968), p. 85.

34. That is, if I turn into a bug's arm will I "know" it and thus be aware of my new form and "enjoy" my immortality?

35. See Ch'en, 1973.

36. Waley, 1934, p. 162. Curiously, Waley translates these characters the other way in chapter 52, where he has, "And he who has known the sons Will hold all the tighter to the mother, and to the end of his days suffer no harm." For more on the phrase *mo-shen pu-tai*, see Ch'en, 1973, pp. 231–47.

37. Lau, 1963, p. 92.

38. *"Tien-hisa"* (literally "all under heaven") can be translated as "empire" and is often translated that way in the *Lao-tzu*. But there was no empire in China before 221 B.C., so I have translated *tien-hisa*, throughout, as "the world" or "the whole land."

39. Rulers in early China referred to themselves as "The Orphan," "The Widower," or "The One Without Grain" (line 15) as a way of identifying themselves with the lot of the poor and unfortunate, whose welfare was said to be the ruler's foremost concern.

40. Both lines are from Chan, 1963, p. 170.

41. Although the final *i* can be read to mean the same thing as the instrumental *i*, since the author uses the instrumental *i* in all cases in lines 2–6 and the final *i* in all cases in lines 8–12, it would appear that a distinction is being made. Accordingly, D. C. Lau (1982, p. 191) treats the *i* in lines 8–12 as the verb "to stop," and translates: "It will mean that not knowing when to stop in being limpid heaven will split; It will mean that not knowing when to stop in being settled earth will sink;" and so on. I dislike the fact that this seemingly makes *i* into a transitive verb (literally, "If Heaven did not stop its clarity"), a sense in which it is never used to my knowledge. But it is possible, I think, to read the *i* in its sense as "and that's all" and go on from there. This would give us the following lines:

8 If Heaven did not have it *(t'ien wu i)*, its clarity, I'm afraid, would shatter *(ch'ing chiang k'ung lieh)*;

9 If the Earth did not have it, its stability, I'm afraid, would let go;

10　If the gods did not have it, their divinity, I'm afraid, would come to an end.

11　If valleys did not have it, their fullness, I'm afraid, would dry up.

12　And if marquises and kings did not have it, their nobility, being so high, I'm afraid, would topple.

Apart from the fact that this gives us the awkward arrangement of having Heaven's "clarity" shatter instead of Heaven itself, there is another reason why this will not work. The reason is that in line 12, while the word "noble" is preceded by the final *i*, the word "high" is preceded by the instrumental *i*, and since it becomes clear in lines 13 and 14 that "noble" and "high" are treated in a parallel way, it seems best to assume that in all cases it is the instrumental *i* that is intended throughout. Moreover, reading the final *i* as the instrumental *i* in lines 8–12 clearly gives us the most sensible reading of those lines.

William Boltz, in his article on this chapter (Boltz, 1985), essentially agrees with D. C. Lau's interpretation of these lines. Boltz reads the *wu-i* in lines 8–12 as "without end" "in perpetuity," thus translating—"Should Heaven remain clear in perpetuity, it might, we fear, split apart; should Earth remain steadfast in perpetuity, it might, we fear, burst open." He points out that this interpretation is supported in the Ho-shang Kung commentary, where *wu-i* is understood as *wu-i shih*, "time without end" (a point also noted by Cheng Liang-shu [Cheng, part IV, p. 40]), and further argues that this interpretation makes better sense of the philosophical message of the chapter, which is that all things must incorporate something of their opposites: Heaven must be murky as well as clear, and rulers must accept lowliness along with their exalted status, anything wanting to be, in perpetuity, one thing only will come to an end.

I remain unconvinced. Lines 8–12 clearly demonstrate what will happen if the actions noted in lines 1–6 are not so. And the point here is the same as that of chapter 22, that the Sage-ruler should model himself on all other things and hold on to the One, which means that he should be simple, humble, and unpretentious. That Ho-shang Kung interprets these lines in this way is not *sure* evidence that this is what the text he was using said: Chinese textual commentators delight in using things said in a text as a springboard to make their own philosophical points. Philologically speaking, I should think that if *wu-i* here did mean "in perpetuity," the word order would then have to be *t'ien ch'ing wu-i* ("Heaven clear without end," etc.) instead of *t'ien wu-i ch'ing*. Finally, Boltz does not explain for the reader why the word "high" in line 12 is preceded by the instrumental *i* and not the final *i*.

42. Chan, 1963, p. 170.

43. On this argument see for example the words of Kao Yen-ti cited in Chiang, 1973, p. 263.

44. Lau, 1982, p. 193. One of the arguments used in favor of this interpretation has always been the fact that the words "perfect praise has no praise" occur in chapter 18 of the *Chuang-tzu*, followed almost directly by lines that echo the first part of *Lao-tzu* chapter 39. Burton Watson's translation of the relevant lines is "perfect praise knows no praise," followed by "The inaction of Heaven is its purity, the inaction of earth is its peace" (Watson, 1968, p. 191).

45. Cheng, part IV, p. 43. Cheng proposes that wise rulers will look upon their large numbers of carriages as though they had none, just as they refer to themselves as people without any grain even though they own all there is. This again is making the base the root of the noble, as is preferring to be like common stone (but in that way remaining firm and long lasting) instead of rich jade.

46. Hsü, 1985, p. 11.

47. Lau, 1982, p. 63.

48. See Chiang, 1973, pp. 282–83.

49. Hsü, 1985, p. 18.

50. Lau, 1982, p. 201.

51. See, for example, Hsü, 1985, p. 19.

52. Chan, 1963, p. 84.

53. See Chiang, 1973, pp. 303–4.

54. For the four limbs and nine cavities, see Ch'en, 1963, p. 371. The "9 cavities and 4 passes" is the gloss in the Ho-shang Kung text. The definition in terms of the seven emotions and six desires is that of the *Tao-chiao ta tz'u-tien*, vol. 1, p. 42.

55. Chan, 1963, p. 188.

56. The only other place we find *chih* for *i* at this point in the text is in the "Chieh-Lao" (Understanding *Lao-tzu)* chapter of the *Han-fei-tzu*, but Ch'en Ch'i-yu sees this as a mistake for *i*, resulting from the closeness of the two characters written in grass script (see Ch'en, 1963, p. 374). "Also" (*i*) is given as a meaning of *chih* in P'ei, 1971, *chüan* 9, p. 736, and most scholars working on the Ma-wang-tui texts seem to read this *chih* in that way (i.e., as meaning "also"; see, for example, Lau, 1982, pp. 206–7; Cheng, part VI, p. 37; Wu,

1979, pp. 59–60; but Chou, 1984 [p. 188] disagrees). But one of the four examples P'ei cites to illustrate this usage is the line from *Han-fei-tzu* (Ch'en, 1963). In all other places where *i* occurs in the standard text (chapters 23, 25, 32, 49, 60, 65), the Ma-wang-tui texts also use *i*, with the exception noted above in chapter 42.

57. For example, the *I Ching, Mencius, Analects*.

58. On the identification of the character here as *hsüeh* ("cavities" or "holes"), see Chou, 1984, p. 192.

59. For *chiu* ("to save") Text B has *chi* ("thorns"); there is a lacuna in Text A. The most plausible solution seems to be that posed by Wu Fu-hsiang (Wu, 1979, pp. 66–67), who suggests that the two were homophones (archaic pronunciations were *kiog* [for *chiu*] and *kik* [for *chi*]).

60. For *chieh-jan* ("little," "in a subtle way") Text B has *chieh-yu*, and Text A has *hsieh-yu*. Hsü K'ang-sheng (Hsü, 1985, p. 28) reads the *hsieh* in Text A as *ch'ieh* ("to lift up," "support"); *chieh* as *wei* ("infinitesimally small") still seems to make the most sense. The *"yu"* in the Ma-wang-tui texts makes sense both as "have" and as *jan* ("in this manner").

61. See Hsü, 1985, pp. 28–29, and Chou, 1984, pp. 194–95.

62. Chan, 1963, p. 197.

63. Cheng, part VI, p. 47.

64. See Chiang, 1973, pp. 351–52.

65. Waley, 1934, p. 211.

66. D. C. Lau (Lau, 1982, p. 227) does not read line 3 as predicate for line 1; rather he combines 3 and 4 to give "In the intercourse of the world, the female always gets the better of the male by stillness."

67. Chan, 1963, p. 208.

68. For more on the significance of these changes in chapter 61, see Kao, 1978, pp. 211–12.

69. Reading *chu* ("tendency") as *chu* ("lord"), as Hsü K'ang-sheng (Hsü, 1985, p. 44) suggests is certainly possible; that would give us "The Way is the lord of all things." But the characters "tendency" and "lord" seem to be distinct in the Ma-wang-tui texts since in all cases where the standard text has "lord" (chapters 30, 34, 69, 78) the Ma-wang-tui texts do as well.

70. Hucker, 1985, p. 396, item 4,847.

71. Hucker, 1985, p. 399, item 4,871.

72. See Henricks, 1979a, p. 177.

73. See Hsü, 1985, p. 48.

74. Chan, 1963, p. 214.

75. See Chiang, 1973, p. 391.

76. Chan, 1963, p. 214.

77. For more on this point, see Henricks, 1982, pp. 521–22. Chou Tz'u-chi (Chou, 1984, p. 216) argues for the connection and follows Text A.

78. Hsü K'ang-sheng (Hsü, 1985, p. 50) also understands *chih* in this way, and Cheng Liang-shu (Cheng, part VIII, p. 36) notes that the meanings of the two characters are close. Chou Tz'u-chi (Chou, 1984, p. 217) seems to read *chih* as "to understand," and D. C. Lau (Lau, 1982, p. 237) translates in this way. That is, he has "Thus to understand a state through knowledge Will be a detriment to the state; And to understand a state through ignorance Will be a boon to the state."

79. Chan, 1963, p. 238.

80. See the argument of Yü Yüeh cited in Chiang, 1973, pp. 460–61.

81. See Graham, 1986, p. 82.

82. Chan, 1963, p. 240.

83. Lau, 1982, p. 241.

84. For more on puns in the *Lao-tzu*, see Henricks, 1981b, pp. 67–69.

85. One might read the *chih* here as *ch'i* and read it as the first character in line 7 (*"The* first *of these* is called") save for the fact that a comma appears in the text right after the *chih*. Clearly what has happened is that since lines 5 and 6 both end with the word "treasure" *(pao)*, the copyist placed the *chih* after the first of these *pao*s instead of the second.

86. Wing-tsit Chan (Chan, 1963, p. 219) translates *ch'eng-ch'i chang* as "the leader of the world," and Waley (Waley, 1934, p. 225) translates it as "chief of all Ministers," noting that it means the same thing as *kuan-chang* in chapter 28. My sense is that *ch'eng-ch'i* does ultimately mean officials or ministers, but that literally it says something like "those with complete (or perfect) talent."

87. See Chiang, 1973, p. 406.

88. Lau, 1982, p. 147. For more on this point, see Chiang, 1973, pp. 415–16, and Cheng, part VIII, p. 42.

89. Lau, 1982, p. 247.

90. Chan, 1963, p. 222.

91. For more on the grammatical precision of the Ma-wang-tui texts, see Henricks, 1979a, pp. 182–86.

92. Chan, 1963, p. 225.

93. Lau, 1982, p. 251.

94. Wu, 1979, pp. 134–35.

95. Text A has *jo min heng shih ssu tse erh wei che wu chiang* (literally "If people constantly affirm death then and yet those who act, I would"). My guess would be that the *shih* ("affirm") in place of *wei* ("fear") is a mistake based on form: the two characters look alike even in modern script. The copyist then skipped ahead to line 4 in which the *tse* ("then") comes right after the *ssu* ("death"). His eye then returned to line 3, writing down the *erh* ("and yet"), but he left the *ch'i* ("abnormally") out.

96. Lau, 1982, pp. 253–54. See also Hsü, 1985, pp. 65–66.

97. Chan, 1963, p. 230.

98. Chou Tz'u-chi (Chou, 1984, p. 237) and Hsü K'ang-sheng (Hsü, 1985, p. 68) agree in reading the unknown characters we find here (i.e., the character *heng* plus the "grass" radical in Text A and *heng* plus the "bone" radical in Text B) as *keng* (the character *heng* plus the "wood" radical) which is defined in the *Shuo-wen chieh-tzu* as *ching* "in the end." They also agree in reading *jen* ("eight feet"— Text B has *hsin*, "sincerity") as *shen*, meaning "stretched out straight" (as the limbs are in death).

99. Chou, 1984, p. 238.

100. It is not entirely clear what the two characters are that are missing at this point in Text B; especially since Text A has *three* characters—*yu i ch'ü* ("have in order to take and")—in the text at this point. But the meaning seems unaffected by our choice.

101. Line 1 in Text A is *t'ien-hsia* □ □ □ □ □ *che yeh*. There are a number of ways to fill in the blanks, one of which would be to assume that *t'ien-hsia* is correct, that is, *t'ien-hsia chih tao yu chang-kung che yeh*—"The Way of the world is like the stretching of a bow." I prefer the following reconstruction, which assumes the copyist mistakenly wrote *hsia* instead of *chih*: *t'ien chih tao ch'i yu chang-kung che yeh*—"The Way of Heaven, it's like the stretching of a bow." This is essentially the reading of the line that we find in the Fu I text (which is *t'ien chih tao ch'i yu chang-kung che yü* [= *yeh-hu*]).

102. Chiang, 1973, p. 454.

103. In an earlier reading of this chapter, I understood the last line of 78 to actually be the first line of 79, in which case it would read, "Words of correction have the opposite effect." See Henricks, 1982, pp. 522–23.

104. Chiang, 1973, p. 456.

105. See Cheng, part IX, pp. 36–37.

106. Kao Heng earlier made the same point. See Cheng, part IX, p. 36.

107. The standard text has *tao k'o tao fei ch'ang tao*; the Ma-wang-tui texts have *tao k'o tao yeh fei heng tao yeh*. I read the first *yeh* as equivalent to the nominalizing particle *che* ("the one who" or "the one which"); *k'o tao yeh* therefore means "the one that can be talked about." Most Chinese commentators seem to understand these lines in this way (i.e., they punctuate *tao, k'o-tao yeh fei heng tao yeh*). See for example Hsü, 1985, pp. 74–75. D. C. Lau (Lau, 1982, p. 267) translates these lines in a slightly different way. He has "The Way can be spoken of, But it will not be the constant way; The name can be named, But it will not be the constant name." In my review of Lau's translation (Henricks, 1984) I took issue with this interpretation: I still feel the first part of each line must be a nominal phrase that is then negated in the second part with the *fei*. On this point also note Cheng Liang-shu's comments and punctuation of these lines (Cheng, part I, p. 23).

108. I translated this line in much the same way in Henricks, 1979a, pp. 195–96. It is also possible, however, that the intended character is the *chiao* that means "white" or "bright," which would give us "only sees that about it that dazzles and shines." For part of the evidence on this point, see Henricks, 1985, pp. 35–36. The *So-tung hsüan-shu* text of *Lao-tzu* (P. 2584)—which is in other ways similar to the Ma-wang-tui texts—here has *so-hao* ("that which is bright or dazzling").

109. Chan, 1963, p. 97.

110. The Chinese is *heng yeh*. A number of *Lao-tzu* texts have maintained nominal phrase structure of the preceding lines with the added particle *chih* (e.g., *nan-i chih hsiang ch'eng*). See, for example, Shima Kunio (Shima, 1973), p. 56. Without this *heng yeh*, however, those lines remain incomplete, unless we read them in the fashion of Hsü K'ang-sheng.

111. On this reading see, for example, Hsü, 1985, pp. 76–77.

112. The Ma-wang-tui texts *seem* to say, "He brings it about that the knowledgeable do not dare [to act]. If he simply does not act on them, then all will be in order." But I am persuaded by a number of commentators to see the *fu* in this line as copy error. (The punctuation would therefore be *pu kan wei erh-i* versus *pu kan. Fu-wei erh-i*.)

113. For more on this point, see the Introduction.

114.   For more on this point, see Henricks, 1982, pp. 512–13.

115.   Chou Tz'u-chi's argument that *yŭ* (normally "bathe") here for *ku* ("valley") [*yŭ* is always used for *ku* in the Ma-wang-tui texts] means the desire aroused by seeing female genitalia seems forced. *Yŭ* can hardly mean anything other than "valley" or "valley stream" in a number of contexts below (e.g., see chapters 32 and 39).

116.   See, for example, Boltz, 1982, p. 100, and Chou, 1984, p. 66.

117.   Thus I assume the *yu* (has) is copy error for *fu* ("*does not compete with them*"); alternatively, *yu* might here mean "further," with the negative *fu* mistakenly left out. D. C. Lau (Lau, 1982, pp. 275–77) reads the *yu* in this way. But he punctuates the line in a novel way, in a way that eliminates the need for the negative *pu*. His translation reads, "It is because water is not only good at benefiting the myriad creatures but also vies to dwell in the place detested by the multitude that it comes close to the way."

118.   Chou Tz'u-chi (Chou, 1984, pp. 71–72) cites some interesting lines from Chinese medical texts on the process of *ying-ch'i*, in which breath turns into blood and circulates in the body. He also notes that the lungs were both the root of breath and the locus of the *p'o*. I think he is right in suggesting that Lao-tzu had these traditional views on physiology in mind in lines 1 and 2 of chapter 10.

119.   How to interpret the *kua* ("juniper tree") here remains a problem. Chou Tz'u-chi (Chou, 1984, p. 73) ends up with *chan* ("benefit") for the intended word; Hsü K'ang-sheng (Hsü, 1985, p. 87) stays with the standard graph of *chih* ("to rule"). I choose to be somewhat conservative at this point and use *huo* ("to be alive," "revive"), which involves only a change in the radical from wood to water. Note that *kua* is used once again for *huo* in chapter 73.

120.   Chan, 1963, p. 122.

121.   Translated by A. C. Graham (Graham, 1981, p. 224).

122.   The standard text has *ch'i shang pu-chiao, ch'i hsia pu-mei*. I read both characters in the fourth position in line 9 in the Ma-wang-tui texts as *chiu* ("to band or bind together"); Boltz (Boltz, 1984, pp. 200–202) reaches the same conclusion but interprets the meaning differently. Hsü K'ang-sheng (Hsü, 1985, pp. 94–95) reads the character in Text A as *yu* ("distant") and the character in Text B as *miu* ("false") and translates these lines "Its top is not unreal; its bottom is also not extinguished." Chou Tz'u-chi (Chou, 1984, p. 88) reads the *miu* in B as *liao* ("clear and deep").

123.   Translated by D. C. Lau (Lau, 1982, p. 21).

124. Chan, 1963, p. 126.

125. In both Ma-wang-tui texts, lines 1 and 2 both end with the particle *yeh* and thus take the form of equative sentences (X, Y *yeh* = X is Y). In addition, in line 2 where the standard text of *Lao-tzu* has *tu* ("thick," "genuine," "firm"), Text A has *piao* ("surface") and Text B has *tu* ("to oversee"). Chou Tz'u-chi (Chou, 1984, p. 98) and Hsü K'ang-sheng (Hsü, 1985, pp. 98–99) both read A's *piao* as the *tu* that means "the stitch going down the center of a jacket in the back," but then they part ways: Hsü K'ang-sheng (and other mainland commentators) reads this as a homophone for the *tu* we find in the standard edition; Chou Tz'u-chi, on the other hand, feels this refers to *tu-mo*, the central artery in the body for breath. Cheng Liang-shu (Cheng, part 2, p. 17) agrees with Chou Tz'u-chi's identification and further notes that this *tu* and the character *piao* in Text A resemble each other in form; hence the mistake in Text A. I follow Cheng's lead in understanding this here to mean "center."

126. Chan, 1963, p. 128.

127. The Ma-wang-tui texts have *ch'eng-kung sui-shih* here; the standard text has *kung-ch'eng shih-sui*. In chapters 2, 34, and 77, with the same phrase (actually just *ch'eng-kung*), the same distinction is made. This is one of a number of features that are found later *only* in the "Hsiang-erh" group of *Lao-tzu* texts. (See Henricks, 1985, pp. 36–37.)

128. Chou, 1984, p. 127.

129. Hsü, 1985, p. 109.

130. Lau, 1982, p. 299.

131. Translated by Wing-tsit Chan (Chan, 1963, p. 143).

132. Lau, 1982, p. 299.

133. Hsü, 1985, p. 110.

134. Chou, 1984, pp. 128–29.

135. For more on this point, see Henricks, 1981b, pp. 61–62.

136. Hsü, 1985, p. 111.

137. Chou, 1984, p. 120.

138. Chan, 1963, p. 139.

139. Watson, 1968, p. 66.

140. Chan, 1963, p. 141.

141. Chan, 1963, p. 141.

142. Chan, 1963, p. 144.

143. Chan, 1963, p. 146.

144. I follow Hsü K'ang-sheng (Hsü, 1985, p. 115) in changing the radical for *huan* from "jade" to "gate" and adding the "food"

radical to *kuan*. (See also Cheng, part III, pp. 26–27, on these words.)
Chou Tz'u-chi (Chou, 1984, pp. 137–38) ends up with the standard
reading by noting that the Ma-wang-tui *huan* means the same as *ying*
("military barracks") and then arguing that since *huan* could be bor-
rowed to stand for *ying*, it could also be used for the standard text's
jung.

Line 4 in Text B, like the standard text, begins with *sui* ("even
though") in which case the reading "magnificent scenes" seems more
appropriate. But the pattern *wei yu* X, *tse* Y—"only when you have
X condition do you then have Y result"—must surely be preferred
over the awkward *sui yu* X, *tse* Y—"even though you have X, then
Y." And, of course, that reading makes such good sense.

Arguing in favor of *sui* being the correct word at the start of line
4, however, is the fact that *sui* is written as *wei* elsewhere in the Ma-
wang-tui texts (in chapters 27 and 32 in Text A and 32 in Text B).
With *sui* as the opening word, one might then translate, "Even
though he's inside a fortified hostel at rest, he remains ill at ease"
(understanding the *ch'ao* in Text B [Text A has a lacuna] as a loan for
the *ch'ao* with the heart radical that means "disappointed" or "sad").
This interpretation has had support over the years. See, for example,
Cheng, part III, pp. 26–27; and Chang, 1981, pp. 161–62. The point
in any event seems to be that the Sage-ruler rarely, if ever, lets his
guard down and never takes serious matters lightly.

145. Chan, 1963, p. 146.
146. Chan, 1963, p. 149.
147. For more on this point, see Henricks, 1982, pp. 516–17.
148. Chan, 1963, p. 151.
149. The negatives used in lines 7–10 might imply "imperative" readings—for example, "Achieve your result but do not become
arrogant." But the declarative mode seems to be called for in lines
5–6 "The good one [*shan-che*] *does* so and so" and therefore in what
follows.
150. Chan, 1963, p. 152.
151. Chan, 1963, p. 152.
152. Lau, 1982, pp. 45–46.
153. Lau, 1982, p. 313.
154. Henricks, 1981c.
155. Chan, 1963, p. 154.
156. Chou, 1984, pp. 153–54.
157. Hsü, 1985, p. 124.
158. Lau, 1982, pp. 314–15.

159. Lau, 1982, p. 49.

160. See Henricks, 1982, pp. 509–10 and 517.

161. Lau, 1982, p. 317.

162. Nonetheless, there are a number of characters in the Ma-wang-tui texts that have an added radical element when compared with the standard text equivalent. And in most of these cases it seems clear that the character without the radical is the intended word: for example, *ku* ("valley") is always written as *yü* (meaning "to wash"), and *ch'i* ("irregular") is written as *chi* ("uncultivated fields").

Cheng Liang-shu (Cheng, part III, p. 39) feels that the intended word is still "to perish," pointing out that *yao-wang* ("to die young") and *shou* ("long life") are opposites.

163. Waley, 1934, p. 184.

164. Chan, 1963, p. 160.

165. Chan, 1963, p. 160.

166. Chou, 1984, p. 160.

167. Translated by Wing-tsit Chan (Chan, 1963, p. 166).

168. See Henricks, 1981b, pp. 60–61.

169. Chan, 1963, p. 166.

BIBLIOGRAPHY

I. Important Studies

Boltz, William. "The Religious and Philosophical Significance of the 'Hsiang erh' *Lao tzu* in the Light of the Ma-wang-tui Silk Manuscripts." *Bulletin of the School of Oriental and African Studies* (University of London) 45, no. 1 (1982): 95–117.

———. "Textual Criticism and the Ma-wang-tui *Lao tzu*." *Harvard Journal of Asiatic Studies* 44, no. 1 (June 1984): 185–224.

———. "The *Lao tzu* Text That Wang Pi and Ho-shang Kung Never Saw." *Bulletin of the School of Oriental and African Studies* (University of London) 48, no. 3 (1985): 493–501.

Cheng Liang-shu. "Lun po-shu-pen *Lao-tzu*." *Shu-mu chi-k'an* 13, no. 2 (September 1979): 43–51.

Ch'in Wei-ts'ung. *Li Erh Tao-te ching pu-cheng*. Cheng-chou: Chung-chou ku-chi, 1987.

Chou Tz'u-chi. *Lao-tzu k'ao-shu*. Taipei: Fu-wen t'u-shu, 1984.

Henricks, Robert G. "Examining the Ma-wang-tui Silk Texts of the *Lao-tzu*: With Special Note of their Differences from the Wang Pi Text." *T'oung Pao* 65, nos. 4–5 (1979a): 166–99.

———. "The Ma-wang-tui Manuscripts of the *Lao-tzu* and the Problem of Dating the Text." *Chinese Culture* 20, no. 2 (June 1979b): 1–15.

———. "A Note on the Question of Chapter Divisions in the Ma-wang-tui Manuscripts of the *Lao-tzu*." *Early China* 4 (June 1979c): 49–51.

———. "A Complete List of the Character Variants in the Ma-wang-tui Texts of *Lao-tzu*." *Journal of Chinese Linguistics* 10 (June 1981a): 207–75.

———. "The Philosophy of Lao-tzu Based on the Ma-wang-tui Texts: Some Preliminary Observations." *Bulletin of the Society for the Study of Chinese Religions*, 9 (October 1981b): 59–78.

———. "Character Variants in the Ma-wang-tui Texts of *Lao-tzu*." *Tsing Hua Journal of Chinese Studies*, New Series 13: nos. 1 and 2 (December 1981c): 221–34.

———. "On the Chapter Divisions in the *Lao-tzu*." *Bulletin of the School of Oriental and African Studies* (University of London) 45, no. 3 (1982): 501–24.

———. "Review of D. C. Lau's *Tao Te Ching: Chinese Classics*." *Journal of Asian Studies* 44, no. 1 (November 1984): 177–80.

———. "The Ma-wang-tui Texts of *Lao-tzu* and Lines of Textual Transmission." *Chinese Culture* 26, no. 2 (June 1985): 29–43.

———. "Ma-wang-tui." *The Indiana Companion to Traditional Chinese Literature*. Bloomington: Indiana University Press, 1986, pp. 410–12.

Hsü Fu-kuan. "Po-shu *Lao-tzu* so fan-ying-ch'u ti jo-kan wen-t'i." *Ming-pao yüeh-k'an* 10, no. 6 (June 1975): 96–99.

Hsü K'ang-sheng. *Po-shu Lao-tzu chu-shih yü yen-chiu*. Hangchow: Chekiang Jen-min, 1985.

Kanaya Osamu. "Hakusho Rōshi ni tsuite—sono shiryōshō no shohoteki gimmi." *Chūgoku tetsugakushi no tembō to mosaku*. Tokyo: Sōbunsho, 1976, pp. 177–98.

Kao Heng and Ch'ih Hsi-chao. "Shih-t'an Ma-wang-tui Han mu chung-ti po-shu *Lao-tzu*." *Wen-wu* 11 (1974): 1–7.

Kao Ming. "Po-shu *Lao-tzu* chia-i-pen yü chin-pen *Lao-tzu* k'an-ch'iao cha-chi." *Wen-wu tzu-liao ts'ung-k'an* (1978): 209–21.

Lau, D. C. *Chinese Classics: Tao Te Ching*. Hong Kong: Chinese University Press, 1982.

Tu Wei-ming. "The Thought of 'Huang-Lao': A Reflection on the Lao Tzu and Huang Ti Texts in the Silk Manuscripts of Ma-wang-tui." *Journal of Asian Studies* 39, no. 1 (November 1979): 95–110.

Yen Ling-feng. *Ma-wang-tui po-shu Lao-tzu shih-t'an*. Taipei: Ho Lo t'u-shu, 1976.

II. Editions of the Ma-wang-tui Texts

Ch'ang-sha Ma-wang-tui san-hao Han mu po-shu. Shanghai: 1974.

"Ma-wang-tui Han mu ch'u-t'u *Lao-tzu* shih-wen." *Wen-wu* 11 (1974): 8–20.

Ma-wang-tui Han mu po-shu. Vol. 1. Peking: Wen-wu, 1974.
Ma-wang-tui Han mu po-shu Lao-tzu. Peking: Wen-wu, 1976.
Ma-wang-tui Han mu po-shu. Vol. 1. Peking: Wen-wu, 1980.
Po-shu Lao-tzu. Taipei: Ho-lo t'u-shu, 1975.
Yen I-p'ing, ed. *Po-shu chu-chien.* Taipei: I-wen, 1976.

III. Variorum Editions of the Lao-tzu

Chang Sung-ju. *Lao-tzu chiao-tu.* Chi-lin: Jen-min ch'u-pan-she, 1981.*

Cheng Liang-shu. *"Lao-tzu hsin-chiao." Ta-lu tsa-chih.* Part I, vol. 54, no. 4 (April 1977), pp. 23–46. Part II, vol. 57, no. 3 (September 1978), pp. 14–30. Part III, vol. 57, no. 5 (November 1978), pp. 21–41. Part IV, vol. 58, no. 4 (April 1979), pp. 33–43. Part V, vol. 58, no. 6 (June 1979), pp. 42–50. Part VI, vol. 59, no. 1 (July 1979), pp. 35–50. Part VII, vol. 59, no. 2 (August 1979), pp. 41–48. Part VIII, vol. 59, no. 3 (September 1979), pp. 36–42. Part IX, vol. 59, no. 4 (October 1979), pp. 23–39.*

Chiang Hsi-ch'ang. *Lao-tzu chiao-ku.* Taipei: Ming-lun, 1973.

Chu Ch'ien-chih. *Lao-tzu chiao-shih.* Peking: Chung-hua shu-chü, 1963.

Ma Hsü-lun. *Lao-tzu chiao-ku.* Peking: Chung-hua shu-chü, 1974.

Shima Kunio. *Rōshi kōsei.* Tokyo: Kyūko, 1973.

Wu Fu-hsiang. *Po-shu-pen Lao-tzu chiao-shih.* Doctoral Dissertation completed at Chung-kuo wen-hua hsüeh-yüan, Chung-kuo wen-hsüeh so, Taipei, 1979.*

IV. Selected Translations of the Lao-tzu
and General Studies of Taoism

Chan, Wing-tsit. *The Way of Lao Tzu.* Indianapolis: Bobbs-Merrill, 1963.

Creel, H. G. *What Is Taoism? And Other Studies in Chinese Cultural History.* Chicago: University of Chicago Press, 1970.

Duyvendak, J.J.L. *Tao Tê Ching: The Book of the Way and Its Virtue.* London: John Murray, 1954.

Kaltenmark, Max. *Lao Tzu and Taoism.* Translated from the French by Roger Greaves. Stanford: Stanford University Press, 1970.

*Incorporates the Ma-wang-tui variants.

Lau, D. C. *Lao Tzu: Tao Te Ching*. Baltimore: Penguin Books, 1963.

———. *Chinese Classics: Tao Te Ching*. Hong Kong: Chinese University Press, 1982.

Maspero, Henri. *Taoism and Chinese Religion*. Translated from the French by Frank A. Kierman, Jr. Amherst: University of Massachusetts Press, 1981.

Needham, Joseph. "The Tao Chia (Taoists) and Taoism." *Science and Civilization in China*. Vol. 2, pp. 33–164. Cambridge: Cambridge University Press, 1954.

Seidel, Anna. "Taoism." *Encyclopaedia Britannica*, Macropaedia. Vol. 17, pp. 1034–44.

Strickmann, Michel. "History of Taoism." *Encyclopaedia Britannica*, Macropaedia. Vol. 17, pp. 1044–55.

Waley, Arthur. *The Way and Its Power: A Study of the Tao Te Ching and its Place in Chinese Thought*. London: George Allen and Unwin, Ltd., 1934.

Welch, Holmes. *Taoism: The Parting of the Way*. Boston: Beacon Press, 1957.

V. Other Works Cited

Andersen, Poul. *The Method of Holding the Three Ones: A Taoist Manual of Meditation of the Fourth Century A.D.* London: Curzon Press, 1979.

Ch'en Ch'i-yu. *Han-fei-tzu chi-shih*. Taipei: World Book Co., 1963.

Ch'en, Ellen. "Is There a Doctrine of Physical Immortality in the Tao Te Ching?" *History of Religions* 12, no. 3, 1973.

Creel, Herlee G. *What Is Taoism? and Other Studies in Chinese Cultural History*. Chicago: University of Chicago Press, 1970.

Erkes, Eduard. *Ho-shang-kung's Commentary on Lao-tse*. Ascoma (Switzerland): Artibus Asiae, 1950.

Graham, A. C. *Chuang Tzu: The Inner Chapters*. London: George Allen & Unwin, 1981.

———. *Studies in Chinese Philosophy and Philosophical Literature*. Singapore: Institute of East Asian Philosophies, 1986.

———. "The *Nung-chia* 'School of the Tillers' and the Origins of Peasant Utopianism in China." In *Studies in Chinese Philosophy and Philosophical Literature*. Singapore: Institute of East Asian Philosophies, 1986, pp. 67–110.

———. "The Origins of the Legend of Lao Tan." In *Studies in Chi-*

nese *Philosophy and Philosophical Literature*. Singapore: Institute of East Asian Philosophies, 1986, pp. 111–24.

Henricks, Robert G. "The Tao and the Field: Exploring an Analogy." *St. John's Papers in Asian Studies*, no. 27. Jamaica, New York: The Center of Asian Studies of St. John's University, 1981d.

――. *Philosophy and Argumentation in Third-Century China: The Essays of Hsi K'ang*. Princeton: Princeton University Press, 1983.

Hucker, Charles O. *A Dictionary of Official Titles in Imperial China*. Stanford: Stanford University Press, 1985.

Hulsewé, A.F.P. *Remnants of Ch'in Law: An Annotated Translation of the Ch'in Legal and Administrative Rules of the 3rd Century B.C. Discovered in Yun-meng Prefecture, Hu-pei Province, in 1975*. Leiden: E. J. Brill, 1985.

Köhn, Livia. *Seven Steps to the Tao: Sima Chengzhen's Zuowanglun*. Monumenta Serica Monograph Series, no. 20, 1987.

Loewe, Michael. "Manuscripts Found Recently in China: A Preliminary Survey." *T'oung Pao* 68, nos. 2–3 (1977): 99–136.

McLeod, Katrina C. D., and Yates, Robin D. S., "Forms of Ch'in Law: An Annotated Translation of the *Feng-chen shih*." *Harvard Journal of Asiatic Studies* 41, no. 1 (1981): 111–63.

McRae, John R. *The Northern School and the Formation of Early Ch'an Buddhism*. Honolulu: University of Hawaii Press, 1986.

P'ei Hsüeh-hai. *Ku-shu hsü-tzu chi-shi*. Taipei: Kuang-wen, 1971.

Robinet, Isabelle. "La notion de *hsing* dans le taoïsme et son rapport avec celle du confucianisme." *Journal of the American Oriental Society* 106, no. 1 (January–March 1986): 183–96.

Roth, H. D. "The Concept of Human Nature in the *Huai-nan tzu*." *Journal of Chinese Philosophy* 12 (1985): 1–22.

Sponberg, Alan. "Meditation in Fa-hsiang Buddhism." In *Traditions of Meditation in Chinese Buddhism*, edited by Peter N. Gregory. Honolulu: University of Hawaii Press, 1986, pp. 15–43.

Tao-chiao ta tz'u-tien. Taipei: I-ch'ün, 1985.

Watson, Burton. *Hsün Tzu: Basic Writings*. New York: Columbia University Press, 1963.

――. *The Complete Works of Chuang Tzu*. New York: Columbia University Press, 1968.

Yampolsky, Philip B. *The Platform Sutra of the Sixth Patriarch*. New York: Columbia University Press, 1967.

Yates, Robin D. S. "Some Notes on Ch'in Law: A Review Article of

Remnants of Ch'in Law by A.F.P. Hulsewé." *Early China*, vols. 11–12 (1985–1987), pp. 243–75.

———. "New Light on Ancient Chinese Military Texts: Their Nature and Evolution, and the Development of Military Specialization in Warring States China." *T'oung Pao*, vol. 74 (1988), p. 220.

ABOUT THE TRANSLATOR

Robert G. Henricks is Professor of Religion at Dartmouth College where he has taught since 1976. He is a well-known scholar of the Ma-wang-tui texts, with a dozen publications devoted to them in major international journals. In addition to his work on *Lao-tzu*, Professor Henricks is the author of *Philosophy and Argumentation in Third Century China: The Essays of Hsi K'ang* (1983) and *The Poetry of Han-shan (Cold Mountain): A Complete Annotated Translation* (1989).

THE MODERN LIBRARY EDITORIAL BOARD

Daniel J. Boorstin

•

Christopher Cerf

•

Shelby Foote

•

Vartan Gregorian

•

Larry McMurtry

•

Edmund Morris

•

John Richardson

•

Arthur Schlesinger, Jr.

•

Susan Sontag

•

William Styron

•

Gore Vidal

A NOTE ON THE TYPE

The principal text of this Modern Library edition
was composed in a digitized version of
Horley Old Style, a typeface issued by
the English type foundry Monotype in 1925.
It has such distinctive features
as lightly cupped serifs and an oblique horizontal bar
on the lowercase "e."